nolo's

SIMPLE WILL BOOK

by Attorney Denis Clifford
Editor: Stephen Elias

Important:

The information in this book changes rapidly and is subject to differing interpretations. It is up to you to check it thoroughly before relying on it. Neither the author nor publisher of this book makes any guarantees regarding the outcome of the uses to which this material is put.

NOLO PRESS • 950 Parker Street, Berkeley, CA 94710

Important

Nolo Press is committed to keeping its books up-to-date. Each new printing, whether or not it is called a new edition, has been revised to reflect the latest law changes. This book was printed and updated on the last date indicated below. Before you rely on information in it, you might wish to call Nolo Press (415) 549-1976 to check whether a later printing or edition has been issued.

Printing History

New "**Printing**" means there have been some minor changes, but usually not enough so that people will need to trade in or discard an earlier printing of the same edition. Obviously, this is a judgment call and any change, no matter how minor, might affect you.

New "**Edition**" means one or more major, or a number of minor, law changes since the previous edition.

First Edition:	August 1986
Second Printing:	January 1987
Third Printing:	June 1987
Fourth Printing:	April 1988
Editor:	Stephen Elias
Production:	Stephanie Harolde
Book Design:	Keija Kimura
	Glenn Voloshin
Cover Painting:	Denis Clifford

Update Service
• Introductory Offer •

Our books are as current as we can make them, but sometimes the laws do change between editions. You can read about law changes which may affect this book in the NOLO NEWS, a 24-page newspaper which we publish quarterly.

In addition to the Update Service, each issue contains comprehensive articles about the growing self-help law movement as well as areas of law that are sure to affect you (regular subscription rate is $7.00).

To receive the next 4 issues of the NOLO NEWS, please send us $2.00:

Name_____

Address _____

_____

Send to: NOLO PRESS, 950 Parker St., Berkeley CA 94710

swb

4/88

Recycle Your Out-of-Date Books & Get 25%off your next purchase!

Using an old edition can be dangerous if information in it is wrong. Unfortunately, laws and legal procedures change often. To help you keep up to date we extend this offer. If you cut out and deliver to us the title portion of the cover of any old Nolo book we'll give you a 25% discount off the retail price of any new Nolo book. For example, if you have a copy of TENANT'S RIGHTS, 4th edition and want to trade it for the latest CALIFORNIA MARRIAGE AND DIVORCE LAW, send us the TENANT'S RIGHTS cover and a check for the current price of MARRIAGE & DIVORCE, less a 25% discount. Information on current prices and editions is listed in the NOLO NEWS (see above box). Generally speaking, any book more than two years old is of questionable value. Books more than four or five years old are a menace.

OUT OF DATE = DANGEROUS

This offer is to individuals only.

Acknowledgments

Thanks to all those friends who helped me put this book together:

Naomi Puro, Kay Corbett, Catherine and Paul Clifford, Marilyn Putnam (for all her help through the years), and all my Nolo colleagues—Toni Ihara, Stephanie Harolde, Carol Pladsen, David Cole, Keija Kimura, Glenn Voloshin, Barbara Hodovan, John O'Donnell, Catherine Jermany, Jack Devaney, Ann Heron, Amy Ihara, Kate Miller, Bob Bergstrom, Christine Leefeldt, Julie Christianson, and Mari Stein. Finally, special thanks to Steve Elias Mary Randolph and Jake Warner for their brilliant and tireless editing of the manuscript. Also, I want to extend special thanks to Dorcas Moulton, for her help with the cover painting, and especially to Jackie Clark, who prepared so many drafts of the manuscript so well, and so cheerfully.

Table of Contents

CHAPTER 1:

How to Use Nolo's Will Book

A. Introduction

This book enables you to write your own will, valid in every state *except* Louisiana. If you are temporarily residing outside the United States for work, study, travel or military service, you can also use the Will Book to make a valid will.

Using Nolo's Will Book, you can safely prepare your own will, in all normal situations, without the services of a lawyer. You will accomplish all major will-making goals, including specifying who gets your property, and how your children will be provided for. By following the detailed instructions on witnessing and other formalities, you can be sure your will is legal. Fortunately, as you'll see, it is not hard to make a simple legal will.

B. The Human Element

The act of making a will may seem minor indeed in the face of the overwhelming emotional force and mystery of death. The larger questions and meanings are appropriately left for philosophers, clergy, poets, and, ultimately, to you. For many, death surely is a painful subject to think about, to talk about, and, often, to plan for. The ancient Greeks believed the inevitability of death could best be faced by performing great deeds. Christian religions offer the promise of eternal life; preparing for death means preparing to "meet your maker." Other cultures have prepared for death in a wide variety of ways.

However you choose to prepare, spiritually, for death, many practical matters must be dealt with. For example, your property will have to be given to someone, or some institutions. It is no denigration of death, or life, for you to be concerned with the wisest, most desirable distribution of your property. Writing a will is an act of concern, or love, to insure that the people (and organizations) you care for receive the property you want them to have.

Though most people are aware that they need a will, the majority of Americans (about 66% according to a recent article by *Consumer Reports* magazine) don't have one. Why? No one knows for sure, but here are some likely reasons:

• The legal establishment has managed to mystify the process of writing a will. People fear that "making it legal" is a terribly complicated task, and are therefore frightened of writing a will themselves for fear of making mistakes.

• People believe that if they go to a lawyer to have a will prepared, they'll be charged a substantial fee. There's considerable basis for this fear. Fortunately, by using this book most people can safely leave their own property to family members, friends and organizations without paying a lawyer.

• Lurking beneath many people's failure to make a will is the superstitious fear that thinking about a will, or preparing one, may somehow hasten death. Though this fear is plainly irrational, it is often a major cause of people putting off writing a will.

C. Dying Without a Will

Let's pause for a moment and consider what happens if you die without a will. If you don't make a will, or use some other valid legal method to transfer your property after you die, the law of your state will cause your property to be distributed to your spouse and children. If you have neither, your property will go to your other close relatives according to a statutory formula. If you have no relatives who qualify under law to inherit your property, it will go to your state (this is called "escheating"—one of my favorite legal words). Similarly, in the absence of a will, state court judges determine who will care for your children and their property, and also who will supervise the distribution of all of your property. Unfortunately, it is highly unlikely that these results would be what you would have chosen if you'd taken the time to write your will.

D. What Can You Accomplish In Your Will?

In your will, you can leave your property, or your "estate," in almost any way you want. An "estate[1]" is simply the legal term for all the property you own. You have an estate whether you are wealthy or impoverished.

Many people worry that the gifts they want to make in their will may not turn out to be legally binding. This worry is expressed in many ways, such as:

---

[1] A thorough will-drafting vocabulary is contained in the Glossary at the end of this book.

"I'm concerned about legal requirements. How can I make gifts so that I know my wishes will be followed? What's the right language to use to leave my property?"

"I want to make many specific gifts to family and friends. I have pictures, mementos, heir - looms, antiques. How can I insure that the proper people get them, and that no one else can claim them?"

Vocabulary - Gifts

Throughout this book, except where otherwise indicated, the word "gift(s)" is used to mean any property left by your will, whether left to individuals or institutions. Some - times, in legalese, lawyers distinguish between "devises"—gifts of real estate (real prop - erty) and "bequests"—gifts of personal property (everything but real estate). The Will Book uses the word "gift" to cover both types of property.

Using the Will Book, you can be sure that all gifts you make in your will are legally binding. To accomplish this, you need only state your intentions in plain English. The Will Book contains all the necessary technical language to enable most of you to leave your property as you desire. Specifically:

• You can leave your personal property and your home and other real estate to your spouse, children, grandchildren, other relatives, friends, organizations/charities, or anyone else you desire;

• You can provide for an alternate person or organization to inherit your real restate and per - sonal property if the first person you pick to receive the property fails to survive you;

• If you are not married but live with someone, you can leave your partner (mate/lover) as much of your property as you wish.

Of course, by making a will you can do far more than make gifts of property. Here's a general picture of what else is possible with a will from the Will Book:

• You can revoke all previous wills;

• You can forgive debts owed to you when you die;

• If you have a minor child, or children, you can leave property to them to be managed by a guardian until they become adults or by a trustee under a trust until the children reach an age you specify (between 18 and 30);

• You can also nominate a personal guardian to care for your child or children, should you die before they reach age 18, in circumstances where the other natural parent is unable, unwilling, or incompetent to care for them;

• You can appoint your executor, the person who handles your property after you die, who will make sure the terms of your will are carried out;

• You can provide for what happens to your property in the event of the simultaneous death of your spouse or mate;

• You can disinherit anyone you want to, except that state law restricts your power to disinherit your spouse;

• You can provide for what happens to your body after you die.

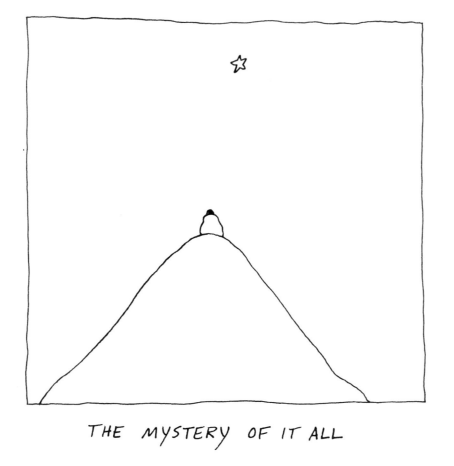

THE MYSTERY OF IT ALL

E. How to Proceed Through Nolo's Will Book

The Will Book is designed for you to read sequentially, chapter-by-chapter. Each chapter takes you through the next steps necessary for you to draft your will. Here's a brief synopsis of what you'll cover:

Chapter 2 contains a general overview of wills—how they work and what you can do in yours.

In Chapter 3 you'll learn about executors and choose yours.

In Chapter 4 you'll review the property ownership laws that apply to your state and make an accurate determination of exactly what property is in your estate.

In Chapter 5 you'll inventory and list your property.

In Chapter 6 you'll specify who are to be your "beneficiaries," or inheritors.

Chapter 7 discusses several considerations that will affect you if you have children. You can skip this section if you are not a parent, and you do not intend to leave property to any minor children. If you have children, however, whether they are natural, adopted, or born out of wedlock, Chapter 7 is essential reading.

Chapter 8 covers the basics of estate planning, including avoiding probate, minimizing death taxes, and using trusts. Estate planning can help insure that your relatives and friends get as much of your property as possible after you die, by avoiding needless payments to governments and lawyers.

Chapter 9 discusses lawyers—how to decide if you need one to review your will, or for estate planning, and how to locate a good one, if necessary.

Chapter 10 contains a discussion of the differences between Chapter 11 wills (basic form wills) and Chapter 12 wills (where you assemble pre-drafted clauses), so you can properly choose the approach that is best for you.

Chapter 11 provides six sample basic wills[2] for certain standard situations. If your needs allow, you can use one of these forms to prepare your own will.

Chapter 12 provides you with more options for drafting your will, including a variety of clauses you may need or want. It allows you to assemble these clauses in a number of different combinations and custom-tailor a will to meet your specific needs.

Chapter 13 covers the formalities necessary to prepare (execute) a valid will in your state, from typing to signing and witnessing requirements.

Chapter 14 covers what you need to do after your will has been executed, from where to store it to how often to review it.

F. A Look at a Basic Will

Seeing a completed basic will drafted from a form in Chapter 11 will help you understand that you really can safely write your own will. At this point, some technical phrases or terms may not be crystal clear to you, but rest assured that every clause and term will be thoroughly explained before you actually begin drafting yours.

Let's take as our example Jane Martinez, a single woman in her mid-thirties. June has never been married and has no children. She has a close relationship with her life companion Michael, has several good friends, and a cherished older sister, Martha Dougherty.

Jane's major assets are the expensive tools she uses in her woodworking business, her sports car, and $15,000 in savings. She also values her extensive library, several pieces of jewelry and one Thomas Hart Benton etching she inherited from her aunt. After proceeding through the Will Book, Jane prepared the following will. It is complete except for the formula language defining

---

[2]The French philosopher Rabelais accomplished the task of writing a one-sentence will, as follows: "I have nothing, I owe a great deal, and the rest I leave to the poor."

the executor's powers (called "boilerplate" by lawyers and included in all wills in the book), and the witnessing clause.

Will of Jane Martinez

I, Jane Martinez, a resident of Monclair, Essex County, New Jersey, declare that this is my will.

1. I revoke all wills and codicils that I have previously made.

2. I am not married.

3. I make the following gifts of cash:

• I give $5,000 to my good friend Amy Wolpren, or, if she does not survive me by 45 days, to my sister Martha Dougherty.

• I give $5,000 to my good friend John McGuire, or, if he does not survive me by 45 days, to my sister Martha Dougherty.

• I give $5,000 to my life companion Michael Francois, or, if he does not survive me by 45 days, to my sister Martha Dougherty.

4. I make the following specific gifts of personal property:

• I give all my woodworking tools and business interest in Martinez Fine Woodworking and my car to my life companion, Michael Francois, or, if he fails to survive me by 45 days, to my sister Martha Dougherty.

• I give my Thomas Hart Benton etching to my sister Martha Dougherty or, if she fails to survive me by 45 days, to her daughter, Anita Dougherty.

• I give my gold jewelry and my books to my good friend Jessica Roettingern, or, if she fails to survive me by 45 days, to my sister Martha Dougherty.

5. I give my residuary estate, i.e., the rest of my property not otherwise specifically and validly disposed of by this will or in any other manner, to my sister Martha Dougherty, or, if she fails to survive me by 45 days, to Michael Francois.

If any beneficiary of a shared residuary or specific gift made in this will fails to survive me by 45 days, the surviving beneficiaries of that gift shall equally divide the deceased beneficiary's share. If all beneficiaries of a shared residuary or specific gift fail to survive me by 45 days, that gift shall pass in equal shares to the alternate beneficiaries named to receive that gift. If the alternate beneficiaries named by this will to receive a specific gift do not survive me by 45 days, that gift shall become part of my residuary estate.

6. I nominate Michael Francois as executor of this will to serve without bond. If Michael Francois shall for any reason fail to qualify or cease to act as executor, I nominate Martha Dougherty as executor, also to serve without bond. I direct that my executor take all actions legally permissible to have the probate of my estate done as simply as possible, including filing a petition in the appropriate court for the independent administration of my estate.

[This clause is completed by inserting the standard Nolo executor's powers provisions, which can be found on page 11:55.]

I subscribe my name to this will this 8th the day of October, 1986, at Montclair, Essex County, New Jersey, and do hereby declare that I sign and execute this instrument as my last will and that I sign it willingly, that I execute it as my free and voluntary act for the purposes therein expressed, and that I am of the age of majority or otherwise legally empowered to make a will, and under no constraint or undue influence.

Jane Martinez

[Will completed by the witnesses signing the the witness clauses.]

G. Estate Planning: Do You Need More Than a Will?

One issue you'll resolve in the course of using this book is whether a will is the only practical arrangement you'll need, or want, to prepare for your death. Although a will is an indispensable part of any estate plan, many people determine they should make some additional preparation, which can include:

• Preparing for the possibility that they will become incapacitated and unable to make medical or financial decisions for themselves. The simplest and wisest method to prepare for this contin - gency is to prepare a "durable power of attorney"[3] (discussed in Chapter 8), naming a person you choose to have legal authority to act for you if you ever become incapacitated.

• Arranging for the most efficient and economical ways of transferring your property before or after you die. This kind of estate planning is primarily concerned with two problems: reducing estate taxes and reducing probate costs and delays. (Probate, very simply, is the court process wills

---

[3]Nolo Press publishes *The Power of Attorney Book,* containing all the information and forms you need to prepare your own durable power of attorney.

must go through.) The basics of this kind of estate planning, which include such devices as living trusts and joint tenancy, are discussed in Chapter 8.

For many of you, a will is all you need, or want. A will has the advantage of being the sim-plest estate planning device, the easiest to prepare. Many young people want to be certain their desires regarding their property will be carried out if they die; they also know it is statistically highly unlikely that they'll die for years. So they decide to postpone the cost and hassles of full-scale estate planning until their autumnal years. A will is all they need for now.

Similarly, the primary estate planning goal of many young couples is to insure to the best of their abilities that their children are well provided for and cared for, especially if both parents should die together. A will allows parents to accomplish this by naming both personal and prop-erty guardians for the children. Later, of course, this same couple may well want to engage in more extensive estate planning if they accumulate considerable property through the years.

Finally, many people, no matter what their age or health, simply do not want the bother and cost of extensive estate planning. They may say, "Yes, I guess I should do some full-scale estate planning, but I never get around to it." Fortunately, preparation of a simple will achieves their basic goal of distributing their property as they see fit, with as little disturbance to themselves as possible. In other words, if you're waiting, or procrastinating about preparing a comprehensive estate plan, be sure you at least have a will.

If you don't know now whether you want more than a will, relax. As you work through the Will Book, you'll take stock of your situation, and learn enough about estate planning so you can make an informed decision about what you need.

H. Will You Need a Lawyer?

Most people can most definitely draft their own will without any aid except this book. The will-making process does not inherently necessitate a lawyer. After all, for most people making a will involves absolutely no conflict with others, which is the usual reason for hiring an attorney. Only occasionally does a will require the sort of complex legal maneuvering that can necessitate a lawyer's skills.[4]

Finally, you should know that no state law requires that a will be prepared or approved by a lawyer.

You also may be interested to know that even if you hire a lawyer to draft your will, the law-yer will most probably prepare it by using a standard will form book containing the same types of clauses you will find here, except the lawyer's clauses probably contain considerable unnecessary verbiage and legalese. Very likely, this standard form has been input into a computer or compu-terized typewriter, so all that's left to be done is to type in your name, the names of the people you want your property to go to, and other necessary information, and then to print out the document.

Some members of the legal establishment have tried to frighten the public with horror stories of disasters that befell some benighted person whose self-drafted will didn't achieve his goals. A

---

[4]Ambrose Bierce defined a lawyer as "one skilled in circumvention of the law."

renowned lawyer once remarked that anyone who can take out his own appendix can write his own will. This analogy is false. An accurate one is that if you can prepare your own income tax form, preparing your own will should present you with no problems, unless yours is an unusual situa - ation (I flag these throughout the book). In other words, drafting a valid will takes intelligence and common sense, not sophisticated skills.

Nevertheless, you should not approach the task of will drafting with an iron-clad rule against consulting a lawyer, or at least having one review your work. Some people's situations are fairly complicated and do call for legal assistance. For example, if you want to impose controls over a piece of land for the next two generations, that requires a lawyer. In addition, the Will Book does not show you how to prepare what's called a "life estate" or a trust, except for a simple trust for property you leave to your own minor children designed to delay the age at which they take the property you leave them. Also, if you believe some family members will challenge your will because you disinherit them, you should consult a lawyer to see how you can best prepare in advance to counter this challenge.

▲ This is the symbol you'll see throughout the Will Book when reference to a lawyer is suggested. Though you'll find quite a few of these symbols in the book, you'll probably not be affected by any of them. Use of lawyers is discussed in detail in Chapter 9.

If you do determine at some stage that you want a lawyer's assistance, this book will still be helpful in a number of ways. First, by having become knowledgeable about wills, and by pre - paring a draft of what you want, you may substantially reduce the lawyer's fee. Second, you'll be better able to determine if a lawyer is dealing with you in a straightforward way, or is trying to bamboozle you into an overly complicated and expensive approach with fancy talk.

One piece of advice. In a will, you are expressing your own intentions. No one else can know those intentions. Sometimes, when people think, or fear, that they need a lawyer, what they are really doing is longing for an authority figure (or believing one is required) to tell them what to do. By buying this book you've demonstrated that you are not willing to turn such basic decisions as the distribution of your own property over to someone else. Good. Keep that firmly in mind when considering whether you actually need a lawyer's help.

I. This is a Workbook

Finally, please treat the Will Book as a workbook, not a book to cherish unmarked. It is specifically designed to help you actively prepare your will. You'll be engaged in the processes necessary to prepare your will throughout the book—writing down factual information, making notes, recording your decisions. A number of worksheets are provided to help you do this. You can leave the worksheets in the book while using them, or tear them out (they are perforated), or photocopy them and work on the copies. This, of course, is up to you. So, take out a pencil, eraser and some scratch paper (in case you need more room than the worksheets provide), and get ready. Without further ado, as speakers at ceremonial dinners say, let's now learn more of what a will is and what a will can do.

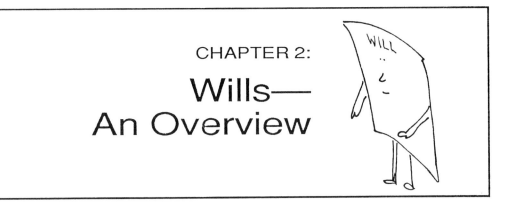

CHAPTER 2:

Wills—
An Overview

A. Basic Legal Requirements for Making a Valid Will

The legal requirements to draft a valid will are not nearly as complicated as most people fear. Read what follows carefully and you will be reassured.

1. The Law That Governs Your Will

Generally, a will is valid in any state in the U.S. where you die, if it was valid under the laws of the state (or country) where the will writer was "domiciled" when the will was made.[1] Your domicile is where you have your home. This means your principal home, where you spend most of your time, as opposed, say, to a summer home. You can only have one domicile.

▲ If there is any doubt in your mind about which state is your permanent home (for example, if you divide your time roughly equally between houses in two states, or if you are in the military and live off base) and how that might affect your will, check with an attorney.

What happens if you move to another state? The short answer is that you should review your will in light of the new state's laws, especially property ownership laws (see Chapter 14 for a

---

[1] Also, if your will is valid in the state where you die, it's legally immaterial that it was invalid in the state where it was prepared.

discussion of what to look for). Fortunately, you'll probably determine that your original will remains valid.

2. Age Requirements

To make a will you must either be:

• 18 years of age or older (the rule in almost all states); or

• Living in one of those few states which permit younger persons to make a will if they are married, in the military, or otherwise considered "emancipated." Also, Georgia law permits anyone 14 years or older to make a will.

▲ Do not make a will if you are under 18 unless you've checked with a lawyer.

3. Mental State

You must be of "sound mind" to make a valid will. The fact that you are reading and under - standing this book is, as a practical matter, sufficient evidence that you meet this test. The legal definitions of "sound mind" are mostly elaborations of common sense. Thus, the standard inter - pretations include that the person making the will (called the "testator" in legalese):

• Must know she's making a will and what a will is;

• Has the capacity to understand the relationship between herself and those persons who would normally be provided for in the will;

• Has the ability to understand the nature and extent of her property;

• Has actual knowledge of the nature of the act she is undertaking; and

• Has the capacity to form an orderly scheme of distributing her property.

In reality, a person has to be pretty far gone before a court will rule that she lacked the capacity to make a valid will. For example, forgetfulness or even the inability to recognize friends do not by themselves establish incapacity. Also, it's important to remember that there's normally no affirmative burden to prove to a court that the will writer was competent. It's presumed that the will writer was of sound mind, unless someone challenges this in a court proceeding—which is rarely done.

A will can also be declared invalid if a court determines that it was procured by "fraud" or "undue influence." This usually involves some evil-doer manipulating a person of unsound mind to leave all, or most, of his property to the manipulator.

▲ If you suspect there's even a remote chance someone will challenge your will on the basis of your mental competence, be sure to see a lawyer. For example, if you plan to leave the bulk of your property to someone you know is disliked and mistrusted by most of your family, work with a lawyer to minimize the possibility of a lawsuit.

4. Technical Requirements

To be valid, a will must comply with the technical will drafting requirements of your state's law. In general, these requirements, which are very similar in all states, are less onerous than many people imagine.

The technical requirements sufficient for a will prepared from this book to be valid in every state are:

• The will must be typewritten (in Section C we discuss oral and handwritten wills), and expressly state that it's your will;

• The will must have at least one substantive provision. The most common substantive pro - visions dispose of some, or all, of your property by making gifts to whoever you want to have it. However, you can also have a valid will which only appoints a guardian for your children and does not dispose of any property.

• You must appoint at least one executor,[2] the person responsible for supervising the distri - bution of your property after your death and seeing that your debts and taxes are paid;

• You must date and sign the will.

▲ In many states, if you are too ill to sign your own name, you can direct that a witness or an attorney sign it for you. In this unusual situation, you should have a lawyer's assistance, espe - cially if substantial amounts of property are involved. It could always be claimed that someone too ill to sign her name wasn't mentally competent. In any subsequent court challenge to the will, the lawyer's testimony that you appeared to be in full possession of your faculties could be very important.

• The will must be witnessed by at least two, and often three, witnesses who do not inherit under the will. This means that the witnesses watch you sign your will, and then sign it as your witnesses. Witness requirements are covered in detail in Chapter 13, Section C2.

Those are all the basic technical requirements. There's no requirement that a will be notarized. In many states, though, if you and your witnesses sign an affidavit (sworn statement) before a notary public, you can help simplify the court procedures required for the will after you die (called "probate"). This use of notarization is called a "self-proving" will and is covered in Chapter 13, Section D.

A will does not need to be recorded or filed with any government agency, although it can be in a few states.

B. What Happens If You Die Without a Will?

Let's look a little deeper into what would happen if you die without a will or other legal device to transfer your property. In legalese, this is called dying "intestate." Unfortunately, most Amer - icans die intestate. Among the famous people who've died without a valid will are Presidents

---

[2]Nevertheless, in most states, even if you fail to name an executor in an otherwise valid will, a court will appoint one and then enforce the will.

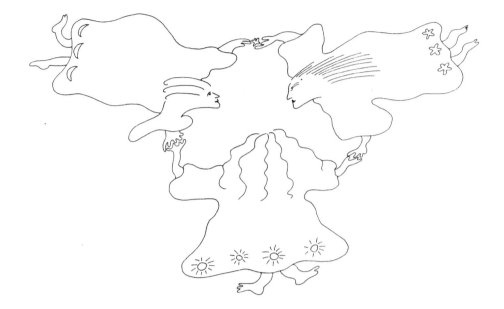

Abraham Lincoln, Andrew Johnson, and U. S. Grant, as well as Howard Hughes and Pablo Picasso.

Since you bought this book, I won't bother with sermons on how foolish it would be for you to die intestate. However, it can be illuminating to understand what dying without a will involves. If you didn't make provisions for what happens to your property when you die, your state law, called "intestacy law," makes them for you. Here's how intestacy laws work:

• A court petition must be filed to have your property distributed under the intestacy laws.

• A judge will appoint an administrator, whose main qualification may be that he is a crony of the judge, to supervise the distribution of your property and hire the probate lawyer.

• Your property (after payment of administrator's, attorney's, and other fees) will be divided as state law mandates. Basically, your property will be parceled out between your closest family members, in different proportions depending upon your family situation and the specifics of state law.

Obviously, the division of property according to state intestacy laws is highly unlikely to coincide with your exact personal desires. If you want to distribute any of your property to friends or organizations, intestacy won't do it. Normally, you don't even insure that your spouse receives all your property if you die intestate since, under the laws of most states, your property (or some of it) will be divided between your spouse and children or other relations. Further, if you're living with a domestic partner to whom you are not married, absent a contract, that person can't receive any of your property if you die intestate.

• If you have minor children, a judge will appoint a guardian for them to manage any property they receive through the intestacy laws.

In sum, dying intestate is as unwise as it is unnecessary.

C. Types of Wills

There are three basic kinds of wills: typed,[3] handwritten and oral. More complicated wills, such as joint wills and contracts to make a will, are generally not advisable for the reasons discussed on the next page. Reciting your gifts, or all the terms of your will, on videotape is not a legal substitute for a valid will.

1. The Typed "Witnessed" Will

This is the conventional will, the kind this book enables you to prepare. Once prepared, it must be properly signed and witnessed. The typed or "formal" will is the kind familiar to courts, and is what most people mean when they speak of a will. (Specific typing requirements for your will are covered in Chapter 13, Section B.)

One version of a typed will is a *statutory will,* which is valid in a few states including California, Wisconsin and Maine, and under consideration in the legislatures of several others. A statutory will is a printed, fill-in-the-blanks, check-the-boxes form. In theory, statutory wills are an excellent idea—inexpensive, easy to complete, and thoroughly reliable. Unfortunately, in practice statutory wills are so limited they are not useful for most people. The main reason for this is that the choices provided in the statutory forms as to how property can be left are extremely limited. And because these statutory forms cannot legally be changed, you simply can't customize them to fit your situation. For example, the California Statutory Will allows you to make one, and only one, cash gift. All your other property must go, basically, to your spouse and/or children. Thus, the California Statutory Will is primarily useful only to people who are married. Even if you are a married Californian, if you want to leave some of your property, beyond one cash gift, to relatives, friends, etc., you cannot use the statutory will.

2. The Holographic or Handwritten Will

A holographic (handwritten) will must be written, dated and signed entirely in the handwriting of the person making the will. It need not be witnessed. Holographic wills are recognized by about 25 states. They are definitely not recommended and not covered in this book. Holographic wills are not recommended because probate courts traditionally have been very strict when examining them after the death of the will writer. One reason for this is that since handwritten wills are normally not witnessed, they are often thought to be less reliable. For this reason, they can be more difficult to get through the probate process because of the need to prove that the will was actually written in the deceased person's handwriting.

3. The Nuncupative Will

This is an oral will. It is valid only in a minority of states. Generally, oral wills, even where valid, are acceptable only if made under special circumstances, such as the will maker's imminent danger of death. Some states impose far more restrictive limits. For example, in California, an oral will can be made only by someone serving in the Armed Forces, just before death, where only personal property is left, totalling less than $1,000.

---

[3]These include wills drafted on a computer using a program like WillWriter (Nolo/Legisoft) or other will drafting programs, which are printed out.

oral will can be made only by someone serving in the Armed Forces, just before death, where only personal property is left, totalling less than $1,000.

4. Joint Wills

A joint will is one typed document made by two people, who are usually married. Each leaves everything to the other when the first one dies, and then the will goes on to specify what happens to the property when the second person dies. In effect, a joint will prevents the surviving person from changing his mind regarding what should happen to the other's property after the first person dies. Joint wills typically tie up property for years, pending the second death. Also, it can be unclear whether the survivor can revoke any part of the will. For these reasons, I don't recommend this type of will. A couple can use the Will Book to prepare two separate wills, which can accom-plish all the sensible goals of a joint will, without its limits and dangers.

▲ If the joint will is regarded as a contract between the two makers, both must consent for a revocation to be effective. This is a potential source of litigation. Be sure and see an attorney if you are considering a joint will.

5. Contracts to Make a Will

A contract to make a will (and leave certain property to the other party to the contract) is valid but not wise. A contract in which you agree to leave your car to Fred will take precedence over a subsequent will (one that breaches the contract) that does not mention Fred and leaves the car to Sam. The usual case in which such contracts are made is where someone provides services—care, live-in nursing, etc.—in return for an agreement that the person receiving the care will leave all or some of her property to the person providing the care. Most lawyers prefer to establish a trust for these situations. Tying up your property so you cannot change your will is not desirable for more reasons than I can list here. Most financial advisors advise against signing a contract to leave property in a will.

▲ If you want to know more about drafting a trust for these purposes, see a lawyer.

6. The Living Will

A "living will" is not a will at all, but a document where the writer states that she wants a natural death and does not want her life artificially prolonged by use of life support equipment. "Living wills," which are also sometimes called "Directive to Physicians," are valid in about half the states. A better way to provide binding instructions regarding use of life support systems is by use of a durable power of attorney (see Chapter 8, Section FG) which is valid in all states.

D. What You Can't Do In Your Will

As was discussed in Chapter 1, you can give away your property in your will in almost any conceivable way you desire. You can leave all you've acquired to your family, a foundation, your favorite grandchild, your lover, or in trust for your cats. You can leave bequests to non-citizens. You can exclude, or disinherit, anyone you want to, within the limits of your state's laws on family rights (see Chapter 4).

There are, however, a few limitations on what you can do in a will:

• You cannot attempt to encourage or restrain certain types of conduct of your beneficiaries. For example, you cannot make a gift contingent on the marriage, divorce, or change of religion of a recipient. You can, however, make a gift contingent on other behavior, i.e., "to John, if and when he goes to college." In general, however, the Will Book discourages making contingent gifts, for reasons discussed in more detail in Chapter 6, Section C.

• You cannot use a will to leave money for an illegal purpose.

• You cannot require your executor to hire any particular attorney to handle the probate of your will. Probate is the process in which a will is submitted to a court, debts paid, and the property ordered distributed as the will directs. While the executor is responsible for seeing that this process is properly carried out, most of the work is typically done by a lawyer (or, more realistically, her secretary)[4] The will writer can informally indicate his preference for a particular attorney, and the executor presumably will follow that request, but the executor cannot be legally bound to do so, no matter what the will says or the testator wants.

Perhaps the most basic limitation on your power to use a will to distribute property is based on the requirement that for a will to be effective as to any particular item of property, you must own it at your death. In other words, a will is not binding until your death. Before then, you can give away, or sell, any asset mentioned in your will. Of course, if you do give away, or sell, property that you've specified in your will, you should rewrite your will to reflect the change.

Also, a will can't dispose of property which you've legally bound yourself to transfer by other means. For example, as discussed in Chapter 8, property held in joint tenancy or in a living trust, as well as the proceeds of life insurance or IRAs, is not subject to a will.

E. What Happens After You Die

After you die your property will be transferred as your will directs, and the other provisions of your will will be carried out. Here is the normal sequence.

• Your executor (called a "personal representative" in some states) locates your will, which you should have stored in a safe, but accessible place.

• The executor hires an attorney for the probate proceeding, unless no probate is required (see Chapter 8 for a discussion of probate and situations where it isn't required).

---

[4]In California, you can handle a probate without a lawyer by using *How to Probate An Estate* by Nissley (Nolo Press).

• If probate is required, the lawyer (or your executor acting without a lawyer) handles the pro - bate court proceeding.

• The probate court officially confirms the executor, issuing her legal authority to conduct the estate's business in what is traditionally called "letters of administration."

• The probate court appoints the persons you named in your will to be guardians for the person or property of your minor children (see Chapter 7 for how you can best control this).

• The executor manages your estate during the probate process, handling (usually without the need for court approval) any problems which arise and paying your debts, including any income, state and federal death taxes.

• Money or property left to a trust created in your will gets distributed to the designated trustee.

• Once probate is completed, your property is distributed as your will directs. Completing probate generally takes at least four months and often as long as a year. Once the proceeding is completed, further creditor's claims against the dead person's estate are not valid.

F. A Note About Will Writing Vocabulary

In these first two chapters, you've been presented with most of the basic lingo lawyers and courts use when discussing wills. Learning this vocabulary and the simple concepts behind it is a significant step towards gaining the self-reliance necessary to write your own will. It's easy to be intimidated and uncomfortable when we don't know what attorneys are talking about. This obfus - cation is often consciously, even cynically, used to keep people dependent on lawyers, particularly with a subject like will drafting.

This book contains a Glossary at the end of the book that defines all the important terms for writing your will and making estate-planning decisions. If you're unsure of the meaning of any legal term used in the text, please turn to the Glossary to aid your understanding.

CHAPTER 3:

Choosing Your Executor or Personal Representative

I t's time to get started making decisions about your will. The first decision you'll make is who shall serve as your executor, and successor executor in case, for any reason, your original choice can't serve. An executor is called a "personal representative" in some states, but for simplicity's sake, I will only use the term "executor."

As you know by now, your executor is the person you name in your will to have legal responsibility for handling your property and distributing it as your will directs. If your will must go through probate, your executor has the authority to hire a probate attorney. If your will is exempt from probate (see Chapter 8, Section B), your executor is the sole person who will supervise distribution of your property.

Obviously, the executor has an important job. Indeed, your executor is legally entitled to a fee for his services, payable from your estate. The fee scale varies from state to state, ranging from a fixed percentage of the probate estate (the total value of the property passing through probate) to "reasonable compensation." In reality, an executor often waives the fees, especially if he is a substantial inheritor of the estate. You should discuss the question of fees with the person you choose for your executor, to be sure the two of you are in agreement.

Your executor's powers and responsibilities are, in very general terms, defined by state law. In addition, all the will forms in this book contain a standard clause defining extensive powers of the executor appointed in that will. This clause is set out in Chapters 11 and 12. When you read this list, the duties may seem so awesome and burdensome that you doubt anyone would want the job, let alone be able to manage it. Fortunately, in reality an executor's job isn't usually difficult. It's the probate attorney (in truth, mostly her secretary and staff) who normally handles the legal details involved in the transfer of your property, unless the executor chooses to handle this himself. With a well drafted will, the transfers themselves are almost always routine. In other words, the people/organizations you specified to receive your property get it without problems. Usually the executor just checks in with the probate attorney occasionally, signs legal papers, pays your final bills and any death taxes (with estate funds), and makes sure your property actually goes to who is named in the will to receive it.

A. Criteria for Choosing Your Executor or Personal Representative

The most important criterion in naming an executor is to choose someone you trust com - pletely. Once you have accomplished this, there is no reason to also require him to post a finan - cial guarantee (called a "bond") to insure that all duties are properly carried out. This is especially true when you realize that the cost of buying the bond must be paid for by your estate. So all wills in the Will Book state that no bond is required of any executor.

If at all possible, your executor should reside in your state fairly close to where you live. Some states require that cash bonds be posted for executors who live out of state, even if you provide that this is not necessary in your will. In any case, because of paperwork and other administrative responsibilities, which may include making one or more appearances in court, it's not sensible to name someone who resides far away from the property and location of the probate proceeding as executor.

Many people name as executor someone who benefits substantially under the will. This makes sense as an executor who has an interest in how your property is distributed is likely to do a conscientious job. Often this person is a close family member, spouse or child.

You also want to be sure to name someone who is willing to do the job. Obviously you should discuss this with your executor, and receive his consent to serve before finalizing your decision.

Finally, you want to name someone who is healthy and likely to be around after your death. To be safe, you should always select at least one successor executor to serve if your first choice cannot.

For many people the choice of executor is obvious—their spouse, or mate. Others select a best friend or close family relation. If there's no obvious person who comes to mind as your executor, you have to work through your possible selections, using your common sense to decide who would be the wisest choice. Do remember, however, that human concerns are usually more impor - tant than technical "expertise."

What about naming a corporate executor, such as a bank? I strongly recommend against it in most circumstances. Your executor is your personal representative in the distribution of your property after your death. You want someone human, with genuine concern, not an institution, to do the job. If your most trusted friend is your banker, name him as executor, but not the bank itself.

However, special circumstances may compel the naming of a corporate or professional exe - cutor. For example, if you are actively involved in running a business, and your executor will be responsible for continuing that business, at least for a while, you'll want someone with business acumen or experience. If you can't find any person you know and trust for this, you'll have to select some kind of professional management firm. Just remember, though, this is a last resort.

What about choosing co-executors? While it is simpler to choose one executor, there is no rule that says you must. There are occasionally sensible reasons for choosing two. Sometimes those reasons are personal—a parent names both children as co-executors, so as not to appear to favor one. Or the reasons can be practical—your preferred choice for executor lives out of state, and you want at least one executor who lives in your state, who will be nearby.

Naming co-executors raises some potential problems. Suppose one becomes unavailable? Under the terms of wills you can make using this book, the remaining original executor serves alone. In case both original executors are unavailable, you should, however, name a successor executor.

Another problem that can arise as a result of naming co-executors is that they may disagree. Should this occur, the disagreement will be resolved by the probate court. Of course, it is wise to appoint people who can work together so as to minimize the possibility of this happening.

Another alternative to dealing with the potential problems caused by naming co-executors is to custom draft will provisions to deal with them in advance. For example, if you think that co-executors are likely to disagree in particular areas, you can provide that one has the right to over - ride the other. Or, if you don't want one co-executor to serve as your sole executor if the other becomes unavailable, you can provide for a substitute co-executor.

▲ Because these are unusual needs, I recommend that you consult a lawyer to review the necessary language you've drafted regarding co-executor's powers.

Note: If you do choose co-executors, you will need to use the "assemble-the-clauses" format of Chapter 12 rather than the simpler format of Chapter 11.

▲ Because of coordination problems, I advise against naming more than two executors. If you have personal reasons why you feel you want three or more executors, discuss this with an attorney.

If you own real estate in another state than the one you are living in, you may want to name a separate executor (called an "ancillary executor") to handle matters in that state. This is because separate estate distributions proceedings must be initiated in the state where real property is located. For instance, if you are living in Nebraska when you die, but own some real estate in Iowa, there will be probate proceedings in both states.

▲ If you do wish to appoint an ancillary executor, see an attorney.

You may decide to appoint your executor to act in other capacities for you. For example, if you decide to prepare a durable power of attorney (see Chapter 8, Section F), you may authorize your executor to be the person to make financial and health care decisions for you if you become incapacitated. Or, if you create a trust for your minor children, you may well want your executor to be the trustee too. Before that choice is finalized in your will, you'll have become familiar with durable powers of attorney and trusts for children, and you'll have discussed all this with the person you choose as executor, and received his or her agreement to your plans.

B. Naming Your Executor

Get your pencil ready. Here you list the name and address of your choice for your executor, and then successor executor. How you'll actually put this into your will is explained in Chapter 11 or 12.

Naming a Single Executor

_____

Executor's Name

_____

Executor's Address

_____

Successor Executor's Name

_____

Successor Executor's Address

Naming Co-Executors

_____

First Co-Executor's Name

_____

First Co-Executor's Address

_____

Second Co-Executor's Name

_____

Second Co-Executor's Address

(if both co-executors are unavailable)

_____

Successor Executor

_____

Successor Executor's Address

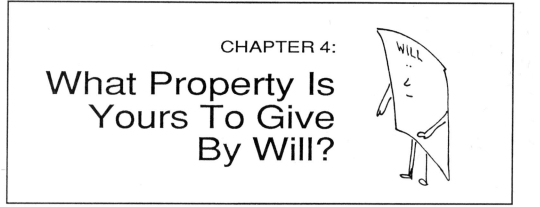

CHAPTER 4:

What Property Is Yours To Give By Will?

A. Introduction

To prepare your will, you first need to figure out what you own, what it's worth, and what you owe. You'll do this in the next chapter. But before you do, it's important that you review the rules governing property ownership discussed in this chapter. There are several principle reasons for doing this. One is that obviously you can't leave property you don't own. In addition, you want to be sure you're not violating any law by giving away property you do own.

What you own is determined by state property ownership laws. Many readers, married or single, will find these laws raise no problems for them. If, as you read the preliminary sections of this chapter, you learn that your property situation is simple, you can skip the rest and move on to Chapter 5.

1. Unmarried People

If you are single and own all your property outright, with no shared ownership, you should have little problem with any state law ownership issues. You are free to leave your property to whatever people or institutions you wish. However, if you own any property in shared owner -

ship—such as property in joint tenancy[1] tenancy in common,[2] or in partnership—you'll need to understand how this shared ownership affects your right to give away this property by your will.

Insurance, pensions and retirement accounts where you have named a beneficiary are other types of property that can't be disposed of by will. I discuss these in Section B, below.

Before you decide that as a single person you can safely skip most of this chapter, do be sure you're single. A surprising number of people are not absolutely sure whether they are married or not. Problems with making this determination commonly occur in three circumstances:

• Many people have been told, have heard, or somehow believe they are divorced, but have never received a final divorce decree to confirm it. If you are in this situation, call the court clerk in the county where the divorce was supposed to have occurred and get the records. If you can't track down a final decree of divorce, it's best to assume you are still married;

• A great number of people believe they are married by common law. Most aren't. Common law marriages are valid only in the following states and Washington, D.C.:[3]

Alabama	Montana
District of Columbia	Ohio
Colorado	Oklahoma
Georgia	Pennsylavania
Idaho	Rhode Island
Iowa	South Carolina
Kansas	Texas

Even in these states, merely living together isn't enough to create a common law marriage; you must intend to be married.

• ▲ Some people don't know if their divorce is legal. This is particularly true of Mexican and other out-of-country divorces where only one person participated. This is a complicated area and beyond the scope of this book. If you have any reason to think that your former spouse might claim to be still married to you at your death, see a lawyer. In the meantime, for the purposes of making your will, assume you are still married.

---

[1] Joint tenancy is a form of property ownership by two or more persons where surviving owners automatically inherit the share of a dead owner. This important estate planning concept is discussed in more detail in Chapter 8.

[2] Tenancy in common is, basically, all shared property ownership except joint tenancy, tenancy by the entirety, and community property. This concept is also discussed in Chapter 8.

[3] This list is accurate as of January 1, 1988.

2. Married People

Married people's property ownership situations are often more complex than single people's because spouses typically own property together. In community property states (see Section E below), spouses typically share property ownership even though only one spouse's name is on the title slip or deed. In addition, as is discussed in detail in Section F below, in the 41 non-commu - nity property states, one spouse usually has a legal right to take a portion of the other's property at death even if that spouse attempts to leave it to someone else.

While these issues are important, there is no reason to become anxious about them. Indeed, if you and your spouse plan to leave all, or the great majority, of your property to each other, it may not be crucial to understand who legally owns each item of property. After all, as long as the sur - vivor will get it all, what's the difference? However, in general, even if you're married, you should know who owns what, and in what proportion, before you make your will. Otherwise, your intentions as to who should inherit your property other than your spouse may be substantially frustrated. How to determine what each spouse owns is covered in detail in Sections D through G of this chapter.

Divorce Note: If you get divorced, is your will automatically revoked as to your (now) former spouse? Not necessarily. The answer depends on which state you live in. In a majority, divorce does automatically revoke a will's provisions as to a former spouse. But in a few states, divorce doesn't revoke the will as to the former spouse. Worse, in several others, divorce revokes the entire will. The moral here is simple: Regardless of the state you live in, if you get divorced, redo your will.

B. Property You Cannot Dispose of by Your Will

As mentioned, there are certain types of property you cannot give away by your will, because that property is owned in a form where a legally binding disposition has already been made. If you try to give these types of property through your will, that gift will be void and of no effect. So it's obviously important that you clearly understand what property cannot be subject to your will. Fortunately, as you'll see, most of these restrictions are obvious.

1. Property Where You Have Already Designated a Named Beneficiary or Beneficiaries

The most common example here is life insurance. You cannot give your life insurance proceeds via a will to someone different than the beneficiary(ies) you specified in your policy.

Other types of property where you normally name beneficiaries outside of will provisions include pension plans, retirement benefits (public, corporate or private, such as IRAs), and certain bank accounts where you add a trust designation (e.g., "Totten trust" accounts or pay-on-death accounts—see Chapter 8, Section C(2)).

2. Property Transferred by Joint Tenancy or a Living Trust

This heading refers to property transferred by estate planning devices (see Chapter 8) designed to avoid probate. The two primary methods are joint tenancy and living (inter vivos) trusts.

Joint tenancy is a form of shared ownership of property in which the surviving owner(s) automatically own the interest of a deceased owner. If you attempt in your will to leave your share of joint tenancy property to someone other than the surviving owner(s), that gift is void and has no effect.[4]

A living trust is a trust created while you are alive, not after you die (i.e., not created by your will). To put it simply, a trust is an arrangement by which property is formally given to a trustee (who can be the owner of the property), who is responsible for managing the property for the benefit of someone else, called a "beneficiary." Property you transfer to a living trust cannot sub - sequently be disposed of by your will unless the living trust is terminated by you prior to your death.

3. Property Controlled By Binding Contractual Agreements

Property specifically controlled and limited by a contract cannot be disposed of in violation of that contract's terms. A common example is a partnership interest. The partnership agreement (a contract) may impose limits on your ability to dispose of your interest by will. For example, the surviving partners may have the right to buy a deceased partner's interest at a "fair market value." The deceased partner can, of course, specify in her will who is to receive the money obtained from this sale.

C. Gifts to Charities

Here's another bit of law you may need to know regarding legal limits on your ability to give away your property—restrictions on gifts to charities. These laws are a holdover from centuries past. It used to be that gifts to charitable institutions (e.g., churches, hospitals, educational institutions) could not be made:

(1) within a certain time prior to death (e.g., within a year), or

(2) in excess of a certain percentage of a total estate. These rules were enacted primarily to discourage churches and other charitable organizations from using unfair means, such as promising elderly people a place in heaven, to fill their own coffers at the expense of a surviving family. While most states have entirely done away with these restrictions, a few have not. These are:

District of Columbia	Mississippi
Florida	Montana
Georgia	Ohio
Idaho	

---

[4]Unless all joint tenants die simultaneously, discussed in Chapter 5, Section J.

▲ If you are in one of these states, you should check with an attorney if you desire to leave a large part of your estate (certainly more than half) to a charitable institution, especially if you believe your spouse or children will object or that you may not have too long to live at the time you make your will. However, if you are leaving a relatively small percentage of your estate to charity, you need not worry about these restrictions no matter where you live.

D. Marital Property Ownership Laws

As noted, many issues of property ownership at death involve marriage rights and laws. Why is marriage so crucial to the rules covering how you can leave your property (by the way, why don't they mention this in romantic Hollywood movies or love songs)? For two reasons:

• First, your spouse may already own some property you believe is yours.

• Second, your spouse may have rights to inherit a share of your property, whether you like it or not.

In both situations, state law determines what is yours to leave by will and what is not. This means that if you are married (this includes everyone who has not received a final decree of divorce), it's important that you understand the marital property laws:

• Of the state where you are domiciled (permanently living, i.e., your home), and

• Of any state where you own real estate. This is important because the marital ownership laws applicable to real estate are the laws of the state where the real estate itself is located, no matter where you live.

▲ A valid prenuptial contract can vary the normal marital property law of your state as you and your spouse agree in the contract. If you have such a contract and are in doubt as to how its pro - visions affect your right to leave property in your will, see a lawyer.

States can be broadly divided into two types for the purpose of deciding what is in your estate when you die:

• Community property states, and

• Common law property states.

If you live (or own real estate) in a community property state, you should read Section E. If you live (or own real estate) in a common law state, you should read Section F. Most readers need not read both sections. If you have moved, while married, from a community property state to a common law state, or vice versa, also read Section G of this chapter.

Community Property States	**Common Law States**
Arizona	All other states
California	(and the District of
Idaho	Columbia) except
Nevada	Louisiana
New Mexico	
Texas	
Washington	
Wisconsin[5]	

E. Marital Property in Community Property States

Reminder: Only married people who live or own real estate in a community property state need read this.

The basic rule of community property law is simple: During a marriage all property acquired by either spouse is owned in equal half shares by each spouse, except for property received by one spouse by gift or inheritance. This marital property concept derives from the ancient marriage laws of some European peoples, including the Visagoths, passing eventually to Spain, and through Spanish explorers and settlers, to some Western states. More recently, in a somewhat different form, this concept has been adopted by Wisconsin.

The other type of ownership possible in community property states is "separate property," that is, property owned entirely by one person. A married person residing in a community property state can own separate property. For example, property owned before a marriage remains separate property even after the marriage. Also, property can be given as "separate property" to one spouse by a will or gift.

Thus, in community property states, what you own typically consists of all of your separate property and one-half of the property owned as community property with your spouse. Together, this is the property you can leave in your will. Obviously, then, it's extremely important that you know what property falls in the community property category and what is legally classifiable as your separate property.

For many couples who have been married a number of years, determining what is community property and what is separate is relatively easy. The lion's share is community, as most, or all, property owned before marriage is long gone and neither spouse has inherited or been given any substantial amount of separate property. Still, even if you believe this is your situation, I recom - mend that you take a moment to read the next few pages to be sure.

---

[5]Although the terminology is different, Wisconsin has recently adopted a marital property act much like those found in community property states.

1. Community Property Defined

The following property is community property:

• All employment income received by either spouse during the course of the marriage;[6]

• All property acquired with employment income received by either spouse during the course of the marriage (but not with income received during a permanent separation);

• All property which, despite originally being separate property, is transformed into communi - ty property under the laws of your state. This transformation can occur in several ways, including when one spouse makes a gift of separate property to the community (e.g., changing the deed of a separately-owned home to community property) or when separate property gets so mixed together with community property that it's no longer possible to tell the difference (lawyers call this "commingling").

The one major exception to these rules is that all community property states, except Washing - ton, allow spouses to treat income earned after marriage as separate property if they sign a written agreement to do so and then actually keep it separate (as in separate bank accounts). Most people don't do this, but it does happen.

2. Separate Property Defined

All property owned by either spouse prior to marriage, or property one spouse receives after marriage by gift[7] or inheritance, is separate property as long as the spouse in question keeps this property separate and doesn't mix (commingle) it with community property. As mentioned, if commingling occurs, separate property may turn into community property.

There are some differences between community property states regarding classification of certain types of property. One of the biggest is that in California, Arizona, Nevada, New Mexico and Washington, any income from separate property during a marriage is also separate property. In Texas and Idaho, income derived from separate property during a marriage is considered community property.[8]

Pension Note: Generally, pensions are considered to be community property, at least the proportion of them attributable to earnings during the marriage. However, certain major federal pension programs, including Social Security and Railroad Retirement, are not considered community property because federal law considers them to be the separate property of the employee. Military and private employment pensions, on the other hand, are considered to be community property.

---

[6]This generally only refers to the period when the parties are living together as husband and wife. From the time spouses permanently separate, most community property states consider newly-acquired income and property as the separate property of the spouse receiving it.

[7]Community property can be transformed into separate property and vice versa by means of gifts between spouses. Further, one spouse's separate property can be given to the other spouse as his separate property. The rules for how to do this differ from state to state. The trend is to require that this sort of gift be made in writing.

[8]Wisconsin's statutes on this point are new and confusing; if this point matters to you, see a Wisconsin lawyer.

3. Examples Illustrating Community and Separate Property Ownership

Many, indeed most, married couples have little difficulty determining what is community property. But if there's any confusion or uncertainty, it's best to resolve it while both spouses are still living. After you discuss and resolve any problems, you should write out and sign a "Marital Property Agreement" setting forth your determinations[9]

Here are some examples to help you and your spouse better understand how community property principles apply to your property.

Example 1: You are living in a community property state and your property consists of the following:

• A computer inherited by your spouse during marriage;

• A car you purchased prior to marriage;

• A boat, owned and registered in your name, which was purchased during your marriage with your income;

• A family home, which the deed states that you and your wife own as "husband and wife" and which was also purchased with your earnings.

Your net "estate" (all the property you are free to give away at death) consists of the car, one-half the boat and one-half your equity in your family home. Why? The car was yours before the marriage and is thus separate property; the boat was purchased with community property income (i.e., income earned during the marriage); and the home was both purchased with community property income and is owned as husband and wife. The computer, on the other hand, was inherited by your spouse and is therefore her separate property.

Example 2: James is married to Sue Ellen. They have three minor children, Peter (15), Sharon (12) and Pilar (10). James and Sue Ellen live in Arizona, a community property state. They own approximately $50,000 equity in a house (with a market value of $150,000) as "husband and wife" and a joint tenancy savings account containing $15,000. James separately owns a fishing cabin in Colorado worth $12,000, which he inherited from his father, and an Austin Healy sports car worth approximately $10,000, which he purchased before he was married. In addition, James owns several expensive items received as gifts, including a Leica 35mm SLR camera ($1,000), a stamp collection ($8,500) and a custom-built computer ($12,000).

Note: Remember, gifts and inheritances received by one spouse after marriage are the separate property of that spouse.

Using the Will Book, James makes the following property disposition:

• His one-half interest in the community property home to Sue Ellen (valued at $25,000, or one-half of the equity);

• His separate property fishing cabin to Sue Ellen;

• His separate property Austin Healy to his brother Bob;

• His separate property camera to his daughter Sharon;

• His separate property stamp collection to his daughter Pilar, and

---

[9]Sample agreements for Californians are contained in *California Marriage and Divorce Law* by Warner, Ihara and Elias (Nolo Press).

• His separate property computer to his son Peter.

James makes no provision for his share of the joint tenancy savings account since this passes automatically to Sue Ellen because of her "right of survivorship" (see Chapter 8).

In addition, James would want to appoint someone as "personal guardian" for the minor children in the event he and Sue Ellen die simultaneously or for some other reason Sue Ellen is unable to perform this task. This is discussed in Chapter 7.

For those of you who may have more complex ownership problems, let's look deeper into how community property laws operate. Again, you won't need to pursue this subject any further if:

1. You are clear about which of your property is separate property and which is community property; or

2. You and your spouse are leaving all or most of their property to each other, in which case it doesn't make any real difference as to whether property is classified as separate or community.

However, if neither is true for you, then it's important to read further.

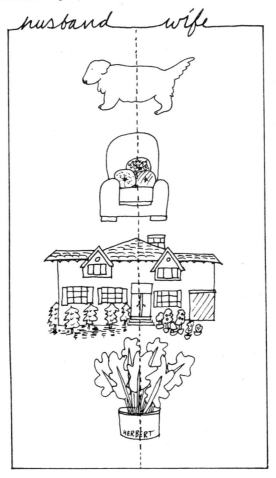

COMMUNITY PROPERTY

4. Community/Separate Property Ownership Problems

In some situations, determining what is community property and what is separate property is neither obvious nor easy. Divorce courts churn out an endless stream of decisions regarding the nuances of community property rules. Here are several potential problem areas:

Appreciated Property: In most community property states when the separate property of one spouse goes up in value the appreciation is also separate property. However, if one spouse owns separate property before a marriage, but both spouses contribute to the costs for maintaining or improving that property during the marriage, and the property has substantially appreciated in value, it can be difficult to determine what percentage of the current value of the property is separate property and what is community property.

The most common instance of this is a house originally owned by one spouse. Then for a length of time, say 10 or 30 years, both spouses pay, from community funds, the costs for main - taining the house (mortgage, insurance, upkeep, etc.). Over the length of the marriage, the value of the house grows tremendously. How can the spouses determine what portion of the present value is community property? Basically, the spouses can accomplish this by agreeing on any division they decide is fair. If they do, they should reduce this understanding to writing. If you can't do this on your own, see a lawyer. Resolving this issue is especially important if either of the spouses plan to leave a substantial portion of the house to someone other than the other spouse.

Businesses: Family-owned businesses can create difficult problems, especially if the business was owned in whole or part before marriage by one spouse and grew later. As with home owner - ship, the basic problem is to figure out whether the increased value is community or separate property. Lawyers normally approach the problem like this: if both spouses work in the business, then the increase in value which the business undergoes during such period is usually community property. However, if only the spouse who originally owned the business as separate property works in it, it is often not so clear whether the increase in value of a business was due to the work of that spouse (community property) or whether the separate property business would have grown just as much anyway. If the latter is true, the increase in value could be separate property in most community property states, except Texas and Idaho, where it would also be community property.

▲ If you plan to leave your share of the business to your spouse, or in a way your spouse approves of, you have no practical problem. However, if your view of who owns the business is different than that of your spouse, and you don't see eye to eye on your estate plans, it's important to get professional help.

Monetary Recovery for Personal Injuries: As a general matter, personal injury awards or settle - ments are the separate property of the spouse receiving them, but not always. In some community property states, this money is treated one way while the injured spouse is living and another way upon his death. Also, the determination as to whether it's separate or community property can vary when the injury is caused by the other spouse. In short, there is no easy way to characterize this type of property.

▲ If a significant amount of your property came from a personal injury settlement and you and your spouse don't agree as to how it should be left, you will want to check the specifics of your state's law.

Borrowed Funds: Generally, all community property is liable for debts incurred on behalf of the marriage (i.e., the community). A spouse's separate property is usually responsible for that spouse's separate debts, as would be the case if a spouse used a separate property business as col-lateral for a loan to expand that business. In addition, each spouse's one-half share of the com-munity property is normally liable to pay that spouse's separate property debts. Unfortunately, it isn't always easy to determine whether a particular debt was incurred for the benefit of the com-munity or only for the benefit of one spouse's separate property. Further, in some states such as California one spouse's separate property may be liable for debts for food, shelter and other common necessities of life incurred by the other spouse.

▲ If you are worried about what debts your estate may be liable for, see a lawyer.

5. Additional Resources

Good sources of information if you are interested in pursuing this subject further are *Commu-nity Property Law in the United States,* by W. S. McClanahan (Bancroft Whitney, 1982) and *California Marriage and Divorce Law,* by Ralph Warner, Toni Ihara, and Stephen Elias (Nolo Press).

F. Marital Property in Common Law States

COMMON LAW STATES

Alabama	Maryland	Oklahoma
Arkansas	Massachusetts	Oregon
Connecticut	Michigan	Pennsylvania
Colorado	Minnesota	Rhode Island
Delaware	Mississippi	South Dakota
Florida	Missouri	South Carolina
Georgia	Montana	Tennessee
Hawaii	Nebraska	Utah
Illinois	New Hampshire	Vermont
Indiana	New Jersey	Virginia
Iowa	New York	West Virginia
Kansas	North Carolina	Wyoming
Kentucky	North Dakota	District of Columbia
Maine	Ohio	

In common law states, there is no rule that property acquired during a marriage is owned by both spouses. Common law principles are derived from English law, where in feudal times the husband owned all marital property and a wife had few legal property ownership rights and could not will property.

To protect a spouse from being disinherited and winding up with nothing after her spouse's death, common law states give a surviving spouse legal rights to a certain portion of the other's estate. These laws are discussed in Section F(2). If you plan to leave your spouse more than 50% of your property, these laws will not apply to you and you can skip or skim that part of this chapter.

In common law states the property you own, whether married or not, consists of:

a. Everything held separately in your name if it has a title slip, deed or other legal ownership document; and

b. Everything else you have purchased with your property or income.

Thus, in these states the key to ownership for many types of valuable property is whose name is on the title. If you earn or inherit money to buy a house, and title is taken in both your name and your spouse's, you both own the house. If your spouse earns the money but you take title in your name alone, you own it.[10] If title is in her name, she owns it.

If there is no title document to the object (say a new computer), then the person whose income or property is used to pay for it owns it. If joint income is used, then ownership is shared (gener - ally considered to be a tenancy in common, unless a written agreement provides for a joint tenancy or tenancy by the entirety).[11]

1. Examples of Property Ownership Rules in Common Law States

Example 1: Wilfred and Jane are husband and wife and live in Kentucky, a common law property state. They have five children. Shortly after their marriage, Wilfred wrote an extremely popular computer program which helps doctors diagnose a variety of ills. Wilfred has received annual royalties averaging about $100,000 a year over a ten-year period. During the course of the marriage, Wilfred used the royalties to purchase a car, yacht and mountain cabin, all registered in his name. The couple also own a house as joint tenants. In addition, Wilfred owns a number of family heirlooms. Over the course of the marriage, Wilfred and Jane have maintained separate savings accounts. Jane's income (she works as a computer engineer) has gone into her account and the balance of Wilfred's royalties has been placed in his account (which now contains $75,000).

Wilfred's property (his estate) would consists of the following:

• One-hundred percent of the car, yacht and cabin, since there are title documents listing all this property in his name. Were there no such documents, Wilfred would still own them because they were purchased with his income;

---

[10]Despite the general rule stated here, the courts in most states will not allow a manifest injustice to occur. Thus, if property earned by one spouse ends up in the other spouse's name, the courts may find some way (called "using their equity powers") to straighten the matter out so that justice is done. This often comes up at divorce. For example, under "Equitable Distribution" law of most common law property states, the court has power to divide marital property fairly (often equally) no matter what the ownership document says.

[11]As previously discussed, property held in joint tenancy (often abbreviated "JTWROS" or "WROS," which means "joint tenancy with right of survivorship") or tenancy by the entirety (a form of joint tenancy for married persons valid in some states), passes to the surviving joint tenant when the other joint tenant dies. This is called the "right of survivorship." Property held in tenancy in common does not automatically pass to the surviving tenant(s) in common. Instead, the portion belonging to the deceased owner passes under the terms of that person's will, or alternate estate planning device such as a living trust.

- One-hundred percent of the savings account because it is in his name alone;

- The family heirlooms;

- One-half of the interest in the house.[12] However, if the house was in Wilfred's name alone, it would be his property, even if purchased with money he earned during the marriage, or even if purchased with Jane's money.

Example 2: Martha and Scott, husband and wife, both worked for thirty years as school teachers in rural Michigan, a common law property state. They had two children, Harry and Beth, both of whom are grown with families of their own. Scott recently died. Generally, Scott and Martha pooled their income. They jointly purchased such items as a house, worth $100,000 (in both their names as joint tenants), cars (one in Martha's name, worth $5,000 and one in Scott's, worth $3,000), a share in a vacation condominium, worth $13,000 (in both names as joint tenants), and some of the household furniture. Each maintained a separate savings account (approximately $5,000 in each), and they also had a joint checking account with a right of survivorship, containing $2,000.

Scott spent several thousand dollars equipping a darkroom he built in the basement. Hoping that son Harry would take up his photography hobby, Scott placed the entire contents of the darkroom in a revocable living trust (see Chapter 8, Section C(2)) which passed them to Harry upon Scott's death, but which left Scott in control during his life. The remaining property left at Scott's death consisted of antiques and heirlooms which both Martha and Scott inherited from their families.

Several years before his death, Scott used the Will Book to make a will leaving his real estate and some personal property to Martha and the rest of his personal property to Beth. After his death, Martha automatically owned the house and condominium because the property was owned in joint tenancy. Again remember, where property is in joint tenancy or tenancy by the entirety, you cannot use a will to leave it to anyone other than the other joint tenant(s).[13] For the same reason, the joint checking account with an automatic right of survivorship went to Martha outside of the will. Similarly, Harry received the darkroom equipment under the terms of the living trust. Beth received Scott's savings account (regardless of the source of the funds) and the specific heirlooms and antiques which were left to her.

husband

SEPARATE   PROPERTY

---

[12]Although the house is in Wilfred's estate, it would go to Jane independent of the will because of its joint tenancy status.

[13]However, in many states you can unilaterally (by yourself, without permission from the other joint tenant) terminate a joint tenancy prior to death and then leave your share of the jointly-owned property as you see fit.

2. Family Protection in Common Law States

If you plan to leave your spouse one-half or more of your property in your will, you can skip this discussion and proceed to Chapter 5. Otherwise, read on for important information.

At first glance, it would seem there is no problem for married people in common law states when it comes to deciding what property you can leave and to whom. If your name is on the title document, or the property was acquired with your funds in the absence of such title, you own it and can leave it by will to the beneficiary of your choice, right? No, not when it comes to disinheriting a spouse. Suppose, for example, one spouse owns the house, the car and most of the possessions, including the bank accounts, in his name alone and leaves it all to a stranger (or, worse, a lover). The stranger could then kick the surviving spouse out of the house, empty the bank accounts, and so on. Of course, this rarely happens. But just in case, all common law property states have some way of protecting the surviving spouse from being completely, or even substantially, disinherited.[14] While many of these protective laws are similar, they do differ in detail. In fact, no two states are exactly alike.

A SMIDGEN OF HISTORY

Hundreds of years ago, the English courts, confronted with the problem of a few people disinheriting their spouses, developed the rules called "dower" and "curtesy." These are fancy words for the sensible concept that a surviving wife or husband who is not ade - quately provided for in a spouse's will automatically acquires title to a portion of the deceased spouse's property by operation of law. "Dower" refers to the interest acquired by a surviving wife, while "curtesy" is the share received by a surviving husband. When the United States was settled, most states adopted these concepts. To this day, all states except those that follow the community property ownership system still retain some version of dower and curtesy, although some states have dropped the old terminology. These, of course, aren't needed in community property states because each spouse already owns one-half of all property acquired from the earnings of either during the marriage.

In most common law property states, a spouse is entitled to one-third of the property left in the will. In a few, it's one-half. The exact amount of the spouse's minimum share often depends on whether or not there are also minor children and whether or not the spouse has been provided for outside the will by trusts or other means (see Section 3 below).

---

[14]Some states in both categories (common law and community property) provide additional, relatively minor protection devices such as "family allowances" and "probate homesteads." These vary from state to state in too much detail to discuss here. Generally, however, these devices attempt to assure that your spouse and children are not totally left out in the cold after your death, by allowing them temporary protections, such as the right to remain in the family home for a short period, or funds (most typically while an estate is being probated). Accordingly, they should not prove unwelcome to any of you.

What happens if the person making the will leaves nothing to her spouse or leaves less than the spouse is entitled to under state law? In most states, the surviving spouse has a choice. He can either take what the will provides (called "taking under the will"), or reject the gift and instead take the minimum share allowed by the law of the particular state. Taking the share permitted by law is called "taking against the will."

Example: Leonard's will gives $50,000 to his second wife, June, and leaves all the rest of his property, totalling $400,000, to be divided between his two children from his first marriage. June can elect to take against the will and receive her statutory share of Leonard's estate, which will be far more than $50,000.

When a spouse decides to "take against the will," the property which is taken must of necessity come out of one or more of the gifts given to others by the will. In other words, somebody else is going to get less. In the above example, the children will receive much less than Leonard intended. You should understand, therefore, that if you do not provide your spouse with at least his statutory or "intestate"[15] share under your state's laws, your gifts to others may be seriously interfered with.

▲ Put bluntly, if you do not wish to leave your spouse at least one-half of your estate, and have not otherwise generously provided for him or her outside of your will, your estate may be heading for a legal mess and you should see a lawyer.

3. The "Augmented" Estate

In many common law states, the share that the surviving spouse is entitled to receive is measured *both* by what that spouse receives both under the terms of the will and outside of the will by transfer devices such as joint tenancy and living trusts. This is called the "augmented" estate.

Example: Alice leaves her husband, Mike, $10,000 and her three daughters $100,000 each in her will. However, Alice also leaves real estate worth $500,000 to Mike by a living trust. The total Mike receives from this augmented estate, $510,000, is more than one-half of Alice's total property, so he has nothing to gain by taking against the will.

While the augmented estate concept is actually rather complicated (I've simplified it here), its purpose is clear and easy to grasp. Basically, all property of a deceased spouse, not just the property left by will, is considered in determining whether a spouse has been left his statutory share. This means that in determining whether a surviving spouse has been adequately cared for, the probate court will look to see the value of the property the spouse has received outside of probate, as well as counting the value of the property that passes through probate. This makes sense because many people devise ways to pass their property to others outside of wills, to avoid probate fees.

---

[15]As mentioned in Chapter 2, a person who dies without a will is said to have died "intestate." When this happens, there are a whole set of rules in each state about who gets what. The share that someone gets under these rules is their "intestate share." As mentioned above, in most states, a surviving spouse's intestate share depends on whether or not there are children. It typically varies between one-third and two-thirds of the probate estate.

4. Chart of Family Law Protection in Common Law States

The following chart provides a cursory outline of the basic rights that states give to the sur -
viving spouse. I do not attempt to set out the specifics of every state's law here. Also, please
realize that many states' laws are quite complex in this area.   ▲ If this issue is significant to
you (that is, you don't plan to transfer at least one-half of your property to your spouse), see a
lawyer.

I.   SURVIVING SPOUSE RECEIVES RIGHT TO ENJOY ONE-THIRD OF DECEASED SPOUSE'S
     REAL PROPERTY FOR THE REST OF HIS OR HER LIFE

Connecticut	South Carolina
District of Columbia	Vermont
Kentucky	Virginia
Ohio	West Virginia
Rhode Island	

II.   SURVIVING SPOUSE RECEIVES PERCENTAGE OF ESTATE

a) Fixed percentage

Alabama	1/3 of augmented estate
Alaska	1/3 of augmented estate
Colorado	1/2 of augmented estate
Florida	30% of estate
Hawaii	1/3 of estate
Indiana	1/3 of estate
Iowa	1/3 of estate
Maine	1/3 of augmented estate
Montana	1/3 of augmented estate
Nebraska	1/3 of augmented estate
New Jersey	1/3 of augmented estate
North Dakota	1/3 of augmented estate
Oregon	1/4 of estate
Pennsylvania	1/3 of estate
South Dakota	1/3 of augmented estate
Tennessee	1/3 of estate
Utah	1/3 of estate

b)   Percentage varies if there are children (usually one-half if no children, one-third if children)

Illinois	New York
Maryland	North Carolina
Massachusetts	Ohio
Michigan	Oklahoma
Mississippi	Wyoming
Missouri	Minnesota
New Hampshire	Kansas

c) Other

Delaware ($20,000 or one-third of estate, whichever is less)

III. ONE YEAR'S SUPPORT

Georgia

G. When Spouses Move from State to State

What happens when a husband and wife acquire property in a non-community property state but then move to a community property state? California and Idaho (community property states) treat the earlier acquired property as if it had been acquired in a community property state. The legal jargon for this type of property is "quasi-community property." The other community property states do not recognize the quasi-community property concept and instead go by the rules of the state where the property was acquired.[16] Thus, if you and your spouse moved from any non-community property state into California or Idaho, all of your property is treated according to community property rules (see Section E above). However, if you moved into any of the other community property states from a common law state, you will need to assess your property according to the rules of the state where the property was acquired.

▲ The opposite problem exists when couples move from a community property state to a common law state. Here each spouse generally retains his one-half interest in the property accumulated while they were married in the community property state. However, the reasoning of the courts in dealing with the problem has not been totally consistent. Accordingly, if you have moved from a community property state to a common law state, and you and your spouse have any disagreement or confusion as to who owns what, you will need to check with a lawyer.

SEPARATE PROPERTY

---

[16]Arizona and Texas recognize quasi-community property for dissolution (divorce) purposes, but not for will purposes.

CHAPTER 5:

Inventory Your Property

Now that you understand how state property ownership laws affect you, it's time to focus on the basic job of inventorying your property. For some people with small estates or who have all this information in their heads, this will be easy. And of course, if you plan to leave all of your property to one person, you simply don't need a detailed list of all of your property. Similarly, if you plan to make only one, or few, individual gifts and leave all the rest of your property to one person, you may not need to make a detailed list of your property.

Example: Jane wants to leave all of her woodworking tools and equipment to her friend Alice, her car to her friend Amy, and everything else she owns (which includes stocks, jewelry, money, market funds and personal household possessions) to her sister Mary. There's no reason for Jane to list each item of property she's giving to her sister.

In sum, if you find that you already know to whom you want to give what you own, you can skim, or even skip, this chapter and move quickly through the next one, where you'll name your beneficiaries. However, more typically, if you own many pieces of property and wish to divide it among several (or more) people and perhaps organizations, you will want to carefully list both everything you own and everything you owe. A careful use of this inventory chart is also recommended if you suspect your net worth might subject you to federal estate taxation. If you want to get a better handle on this, see Chapter 8.

Listing your property means recording all your property (your assets) and your debts (your liabilities) on the chart provided in Section B of this chapter for use later when you make specific gifts in your will.[1] To help you do this, the property chart is divided into two sections, appropriate labeled "Assets" and "Liabilities." Each of these sections is then further divided into four categories designed to help you identify and value your property. Take a look at the chart now to get acquainted with how it works.

A. How to Complete Your Property Chart

Before filling out the property chart, please read the following brief discussion.

Category 1. Identify and Describe Your Property

The first category of the Assets section of the property chart is for listing your property.

a. Identify Your Personal Property

Your personal property consists of all your property except real estate, i.e., your liquid assets (cash, savings accounts, etc.), all your business property except business real estate, and all other non-real estate possessions you own.

You need to identify the property in sufficient detail so that there can be no question as to what the gift consists of. Here are some examples:

• Certificate of Deposit, No. 10235, Lighthouse Savings and Loan Association, Ventura, CA;

• My savings account at Bay Bank (if you have only one savings account);

• My savings account number #18-17411 at Bay Bank (if you have more than one savings account);

• 50 shares Transpacific Corporation common stock;

• $10,000 El Dorado Drainage and Water System, District of Alameda, 1980 bond series C, 10.5% due June 1, 2000.

Valuable Items: Items of personal property which have significant monetary personal or sentimental value should be separately identified. For example:

• "My 1986 Mercedes Automobile, License # 123456";

• "My Tiffany lamp";

• "My gold earrings with the small rubies in them";

• "My Daumier print captioned "Les beaux jours de la vie."

---

[1]As you complete this chart, it may occur to you that your property, ownership documents and other important papers are spread all over the place. Leaving this kind of mess at your death is almost guaranteed to make life miserable for your executor. Therefore, along with making your will, it is wise to adopt a coherent system to list and organize all your property. For a convenient way to do this, see *Your Family Records: How to Preserve Personal, Financial and Legal History*, by Pladsen & Clifford (Nolo Press).

Business Interests: Remember, "personal property" includes all business interests (except, of course, any real estate, which be dealt with under the real estate clause below). For many people in business for themselves, the business is their most valuable asset. It can, in many cases, be left as simply as any other personal property.

"I give all my interest in Ace Pharmacy to my husband, George Malone, or, if he does not survive me, to my children, Andrew Malone and Alexis Malone."

▲ However, often business interests cannot be left so simply. First, there may be co-owners as partners or corporate shareholders who have ownership, buy-out, and/or management rights which must be considered. Second, there's always the practical problem of trying to insure continuity, or survival, of the business, which often takes far more planning than deciding who to leave ownership to. If you face these problems, see a lawyer.

Less Valuable Items: If you are like most people, you have all sorts of minor personal items you don't want to bother itemizing. To deal with these, you can state that all items in a certain category (e.g., "all my tools," "all my dolls," or baseball cards, or records, or machines and equipment) are given to __whoever you choose__." Or, as another alternative, you can state that "all my personal possessions and furnishings not otherwise disposed of in this will are given to __whoever you choose__."

PORTRAIT OF AUNT ZELDA

b. Identify Your Real Property

To describe real property, simply list its address or location. This is normally the street address, or condominium apartment number. If there is no post office address, as in the case if you own undeveloped land, simply describe the real property in normal language (e.g., my 120 acres in Lincoln County near the town of Douglas). You don't need to use the legal description from the deed.

It often happens that real property contains items which are properly classified as personal property. For instance, farms are often sold with tools and animals. If you intend your real property gift to include personal property, indicate generally what this consists of. It's best to generally specify the large ticket items (e.g., tractor, cattle, etc.) and refer generally to the rest of the items as "personal property".

Example: "My 240 acre truck farm in Whitman County with all tools, animals, machines and other personal property found there at my death, except for the two bulls which I give to my son Fred elsewhere in this will."

Example: "My fishing cabin on the Wild River in Maine with all the fishing gear, furniture, tools and other personal property which is found there at my death."

Category 2. State How Your Property Is Owned

As discussed in detail in Chapter 4, it's important to identify any property that you own jointly with someone else and determine exactly how much of it you own so you know exactly what property you can transfer by will. Or, to reverse the point, it's important that you understand what property is not eligible to be included in our will because it is owned by someone else.

Here are the major types of property ownership and the symbols you should use to record your ownership on the chart. If you have any questions about any of these, refer to Chapter 4.

a. Property You Can Leave By Will

Sole Ownership (S.O.): Property you own solely and outright. This generally includes all property in your name in common law property states (Chapter 4, Section F) and all your separate property in community property states (Chapter 4, Section E).

Tenancy in Common (T.C.): Property held in shared ownership which is not joint tenancy or tenancy by the entirety (see (d)). If the ownership deed doesn't specify the type of shared ownership, it is tenancy in common. You can leave your portion of property held as tenants in common in your will, unless restricted by a contract (such as a partnership agreement).

Community Property (C.P.): In community property states, property acquired during a marriage. You can leave your one-half share of community property to whomever you want to have it. See Chapter 4, Section E). The other one-half of the community property already belongs to your spouse and you have no power to provide for it in your will.

b. Property You Cannot Transfer by Will

Joint Tenancy (J.T.) and Tenancy by the Entirety (T.E): As previously described in Chapter 4, Section B, you cannot normally will any property owned in joint tenancy (often abbreviated as "JTWROS," meaning "joint tenancy with right of survivorship") or tenancy by the entirety. The reason for this is that the share of the first tenant to die must go to the surviving tenant(s). (For more on joint tenancy and tenancy by the entirety, see Chapter 8.) Joint tenancy and tenancy by the entirety must be spelled out in an ownership document. It's never presumed.

In the rare case of simultaneous death of joint tenants, or tenants by the entirety, the property is divided into as many shares as there are joint tenants. Then the shares are divided as if each of the tenants survived the other. So, if you want to be extra thorough, you can make provision in your will for what happens to your share of joint tenancy or tenancy by the entirety property in the event you and the other joint tenants die simultaneously. In this case, you can give your share of the joint tenancy property like any other gift you make to whomever you want to (see Chapter 6).

Living Trust Property (L.T.): Property you own which you have transferred to a living trust. This property cannot be transferred by will unless you terminate the living trust (see Chapter 4, Section B and Chapter 8).

Insurance Pensions, etc. (I.P.): Insurance policies pensions and other benefits with a named beneficiary(ies), such as an IRA, or a KEOGH (see Chapter 4, Section B). You can't leave these types of property in a will.

Bank Account Trusts (B.A.T.): Bank trust accounts (sometimes called "Totten Trusts" or "Pay on Death Accounts") where you have named beneficiary(ies) to take the funds when you die. You can't leave these funds in your will unless you terminate the trust (see Chapter 8).

Most people will be able to quickly determine the legal categories their property falls into. However, occasionally, to be sure about the ownership status of a particular piece of property you may have to do some work. For example, you may have to dig out the deed to your house or stock certificates to clarify if you own property in joint tenancy or not. Never guess! If you're not sure how you own an item of property, take the time to find out. Do this even if it means you have to check real property records at the recorder's office or do similar detective work.

If you live in a community property state and are married you may have more difficult prob-lems concerning property ownership as discussed in Chapter 4, Section E. Be sure to resolve them. For example, if you are unsure whether a $10,000 bank account is community property or your separate property, bear in mind that it matters a great deal how you and your spouse characterize it, assuming you can agree in writing.

▲ If your conclusions about your gifts or the value of your net estate depend heavily on charac-terizations of property about which you are uncertain, you should seek advice from a lawyer or accountant. Otherwise you may end up leaving property you don't own, or fail to dispose of property which you do.

Category 3. List the Percentage of Shared Property You Own

In this third category, list the percentage of each item of shared property you own. You should have just figured this out as part of filling in the information for Category 2. People who own property as tenants in common should be particularly careful, however. Since you can own any percentage of that property—from 1% to 99%—it's important you know what portion is yours. Also, this information is necessary to determine the net value of your property for tax purposes.

If the property is community property or a tenancy by the entirety, the ownership is auto-matically 50-50. If it is held in joint tenancy, all joint tenants own equal shares. Thus, if there are two joint tenants, the ownership is 50-50; if there are three, each owns one-third, and so on.

Category 4. Estimate the Net Value of Your Property

In this category list the "net value" of your property. Net value means your equity in your share of the property, (i.e., the market value of your share, less your share of any encumbrances on it, such as a mortgage on a house or the loan amount due on a car). Doing this not only helps you determine the value of what you have to give away in your will, but also tells you whether you're likely to be subject to death taxes, especially federal estate taxes (see Chapter 8).

Example: If you own a house with a market value of $250,000 as tenants in common with your brother and you each own half, you would compute the value of your share by first subtracting the amount of any mortgages, deeds of trust, liens, past due taxes, etc. from the market value to arrive at the total equity in the property. If you assume that there is a $100,000 mortgage and no other debts, this means that the total equity is $150,000. As you own half of the property, it follows that your share is worth $75,000.

Obviously, listing the net value of your property involves making estimates. Doing this is fine; there is no need to burden yourself with seeking absolutely precise figures. Remember, your death taxes, if any, will be based on the net value of all your property when you die, not its current worth. For example, if you think your solely owned house is worth about $200,000, your car $5,000, and your stamp collection would fetch $2,000 if you put an ad in a philatelist's journal, use those numbers. If these items are owned as community property with your spouse or in joint tenancy with your brother, divide each of these amounts in half to determine the value of your share. It's a most unusual case indeed where you'd need an appraiser to give you a valuation of any of your property at this stage.[2] At most, take a few minutes time to investigate what any particular item of property is worth.

B. Your Property Chart

Remember, this chart is purely for your convenience. It can be as messy as you care or need to make it, as long as you know what's on it when you select your beneficiaries in Chapter 6 and draft your will from Chapters 11 or 12.

After you list all of your property, take a moment to review whether each item can be left by your will. To be sure your conclusions are correct, review the discussion under Category 2 above. Then, for each item you can leave by will, mark a W in the box. Doing this makes it quick and easy to refer back to this chart later when it comes time to actually make your will.

---

[2]Appraisals may be necessary for tax and probate purposes after you die.

Property Chart

I. Assets

Category 1	Category 2	Category 3	Category 4
Description of Your Property	How Your Property Is Owned	Percentage You Own	Net Value of Your Share

A. Liquid Assets

1. cash (dividends, etc.)

☐ _____ | _____ | _____ | _____

☐ _____ | _____ | _____ | _____

☐ _____ | _____ | _____ | _____

☐ _____ | _____ | _____ | _____

2. savings accounts

☐ _____ | _____ | _____ | _____

☐ _____ | _____ | _____ | _____

☐ _____ | _____ | _____ | _____

☐ _____ | _____ | _____ | _____

3. checking accounts

☐ _____ | _____ | _____ | _____

☐ _____ | _____ | _____ | _____

☐ _____ | _____ | _____ | _____

☐ _____ | _____ | _____ | _____

Category 1

Description of Your Property

Category 1 Description of Your Property	Category 2 How Your Property Is Owned	Category 3 Percentage You Own	Category 4 Net Value of Your Share
4. money market accounts			
☐			
☐			
☐			
☐			
5. certificates of deposit			
☐			
☐			
☐			
☐			
6. mutual funds			
☐			
☐			
☐			
☐			

Category 1

Description of Your Property

	Category 2 How Your Property Is Owned	Category 3 Percentage You Own	Category 4 Net Value of Your Share

B. Other Personal Property (all your property except liquid assets, business interests and real estate houses, buildings, apartments, etc.)

1. listed (private corporation) stocks and bonds

☐ _____ _____ _____ _____
☐ _____ _____ _____ _____
☐ _____ _____ _____ _____
☐ _____ _____ _____ _____

2. unlisted stocks and bonds

☐ _____ _____ _____ _____
☐ _____ _____ _____ _____
☐ _____ _____ _____ _____
☐ _____ _____ _____ _____

3. government bonds

☐ _____ _____ _____ _____
☐ _____ _____ _____ _____
☐ _____ _____ _____ _____
☐ _____ _____ _____ _____

Category 1

Description of Your Property

	Category 2 How Your Property Is Owned	Category 3 Percentage You Own	Category 4 Net Value of Your Share
4. automobiles and other vehicles, including boats and recreational vehicles			
☐ _____	_____	_____	_____
☐ _____	_____	_____	_____
☐ _____	_____	_____	_____
☐ _____	_____	_____	_____
5. precious metals			
☐ _____	_____	_____	_____
☐ _____	_____	_____	_____
☐ _____	_____	_____	_____
☐ _____	_____	_____	_____
6. household goods			
☐ _____	_____	_____	_____
☐ _____	_____	_____	_____
☐ _____	_____	_____	_____
☐ _____	_____	_____	_____
7. clothing			
☐ _____	_____	_____	_____
☐ _____	_____	_____	_____
☐ _____	_____	_____	_____
☐ _____	_____	_____	_____

Category 1	Category 2	Category 3	Category 4
Description of Your Property	How Your Property Is Owned	Percentage You Own	Net Value of Your Share
8. jewelry and furs			
☐ _____	_____	_____	_____
☐ _____	_____	_____	_____
☐ _____	_____	_____	_____
☐ _____	_____	_____	_____
9. art works and antiques			
☐ _____	_____	_____	_____
☐ _____	_____	_____	_____
☐ _____	_____	_____	_____
☐ _____	_____	_____	_____
10. tools and equipment			
☐ _____	_____	_____	_____
☐ _____	_____	_____	_____
☐ _____	_____	_____	_____
☐ _____	_____	_____	_____
11. valuable livestock/animals			
☐ _____	_____	_____	_____
☐ _____	_____	_____	_____
☐ _____	_____	_____	_____
☐ _____	_____	_____	_____

Category 1	Category 2	Category 3	Category 4
Description of Your Property	How Your Property Is Owned	Percentage You Own	Net Value of Your Share
12. money owed you (personal loans, etc.)			
☐ _____	_____	_____	_____
☐ _____	_____	_____	_____
☐ _____	_____	_____	_____
☐ _____	_____	_____	_____
13. vested interest in profit sharing plan, stock options, etc.			
☐ _____	_____	_____	_____
☐ _____	_____	_____	_____
☐ _____	_____	_____	_____
☐ _____	_____	_____	_____
14. limited partnerships			
☐ _____	_____	_____	_____
☐ _____	_____	_____	_____
☐ _____	_____	_____	_____
☐ _____	_____	_____	_____
15. vested interest in retirement plans, IRAs, death benefits, annuities			
☐ _____	_____	_____	_____
☐ _____	_____	_____	_____
☐ _____	_____	_____	_____
☐ _____	_____	_____	_____

| Category 1 | Category 2 | Category 3 | Category 4 |
Description of Your Property	How Your Property Is Owned	Percentage You Own	Net Value of Your Share

16. life insurance (payment amounts)

☐ _____ | _____ | _____ | _____
☐ _____ | _____ | _____ | _____
☐ _____ | _____ | _____ | _____
☐ _____ | _____ | _____ | _____

17. miscellaneous (any personal property not listed above)

☐ _____ | _____ | _____ | _____
☐ _____ | _____ | _____ | _____
☐ _____ | _____ | _____ | _____
☐ _____ | _____ | _____ | _____

C. Business Personal Property

1. patents, copyrights and royalties

☐ _____ | _____ | _____ | _____
☐ _____ | _____ | _____ | _____
☐ _____ | _____ | _____ | _____
☐ _____ | _____ | _____ | _____

Category 1

Description of Your Property

Category 2
How Your Property Is Owned

Category 3
Percentage You Own

Category 4
Net Value of Your Share

2. business ownerships (partnerships, sole proprietorships, corporations, etc.; list separately and use a separate sheet of paper if you need to elaborate)

name and type of business

☐ _____

☐ _____

☐ _____

☐ _____

name and type of business

☐ _____

☐ _____

☐ _____

☐ _____

3. miscellaneous receivables (mortgages, deeds of trust, or promissory notes held by you; any rents due from income property owned by you; and payments due for professional or personal services or property sold by you that are not fully paid by the purchaser)

☐ _____

☐ _____

☐ _____

☐ _____

D. Real Estate

Category 1

Description of Your Property

Category 2 How Your Property Is Owned

Category 3 Percentage You Own

Category 4 Net Value of Your Share

address ☐ ☐ ☐ ☐

address ☐ ☐ ☐ ☐

address ☐ ☐ ☐ ☐

Category 1

Description of Your Property

address

_____

☐ _____

☐ _____

☐ _____

☐ _____

address

_____

☐ _____

☐ _____

☐ _____

☐ _____

E. TOTAL NET VALUE OF ALL YOUR ASSETS

Category 2

How Your
Property
Is Owned

Category 3

Percentage
You Own

Category 4

Net Value of
Your Share

$ _____

II. Liabilities (what you owe)

Many of your liabilities will already have been accounted for because you listed the net value of your property in Part I of this chart. For example, to determine the net value of your interest in real estate, you deducted the amount of all mortgages and encumbrances on that real estate. Similarly the value of a small business is the value after business debts and other obligations are subtracted. For this reason, the only liabilities you need list here are those not previously covered. Don't bother with the small stuff (such as the phone bill, or what you owe on your credit card this month), which changes frequently. Just list all major liabilities not previously accounted for, so you can get a clearer picture of your net worth.

Category 1

To Whom Debt Is Owed

Category 2

Net Amount of
Debt You Owe

A. Personal Property Debts

1. personal loans (banks, major credit cards, etc.)

2. other personal debts

Category 1

To Whom Debt Is Owed

B. Taxes (include only taxes past and currently due. Do not include taxes due in the future or estimated estate taxes)

_____

_____

_____

_____

_____

_____

C. Any other liabilities (legal judgments, accrued child support, etc.)

D. TOTAL LIABILITIES [excluding those liabilities already deducted in Section I]

III. NET WORTH [Assets I(**D**) minus Liabilities II(**D**)]

Note: It is this net worth figure which you will use in Chapter 8 to help you determine whether additional estate planning techniques are sensible.

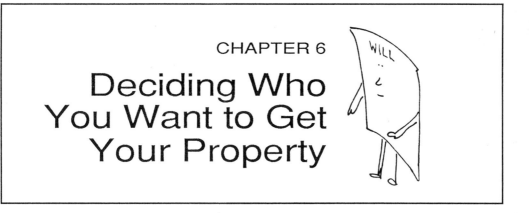

CHAPTER 6

Deciding Who You Want to Get Your Property

Now it's time to record your choices of who gets the property you listed in Chapter 5. To help you do this, I provide a chart on which you will be asked to designate beneficiaries and alternate beneficiaries to receive the following types of gifts:

- Cash;

- Specific personal property items, including business interests;

- Forgiveness of debts (a type of gift);

- Specific real property items; and

- The rest of your estate (called your "residuary estate").

When you draft your will in Chapter 11 or Chapter 12, you will use the information from this chart to guide you in your property disposition.

Deciding who is to receive your property is the heart of preparing your will. Normally it involves making personal decisions, not legal ones. For most people, it's satisfying to make gifts[1] to those they care about. And, of course, it can be very satisfying to know you've arranged to give property you cherish to people who'll value it as much as you do. Before you decide what property you want to give to which persons, some general information about leaving property in a will is in order.

---

[1]For a fascinating exploration of the meanings of giving, read *The Gift: Imagination and the Erotic Life of Property*, by Lewis Hyde (Random House).

A. Basic Terminology

There are several basic legal terms involved in deciding who is to receive your property. Let's define each briefly.

Beneficiary: The person(s) or organization(s) you name to receive your property.

Example: "I give $10,000 to my cousin Sean O'Reilley."

Alternate or Contingent Beneficiary: A person or organization you name to receive a gift if the original beneficiary does not receive it (usually because that original beneficiary predeceases the will writer or does not survive her by some number of days designated in the will).

Example: "I give $10,000 to my cousin Sean O'Reilley, or, if he does not survive me by 45 days, to his daughter Barbara O'Reilley."

Specific Gift:[2] Specifically identified property which you give to a named beneficiary, such as the $10,000 in the previous example. You already listed your property in Chapter 5.

Residue or Residuary Estate: What remains of your property after all specific gifts are made. The will writer's costs for death taxes, probate, and last debts are often specifically made payable from the residuary estate under the terms of the will. Some wills make few specific gifts and simply leave the bulk of their property in the residue.

Residuary Beneficiary: The person(s) and/or organization(s) you name to receive the residue of your property after your specific gifts are distributed and your debts, taxes, probate and attorney fees are paid.

Survivorship Period: The period of time specified in a will that a beneficiary (usually including alternate beneficiaries and the residuary beneficiary) must survive the will writer in order to legally inherit the gift. Between 45 and 180 days is a common survivorship period.

B. Explanations and Commentary Accompanying Gifts

With very few limits, you can will your property however you choose. Most people simply leave their worldly goods to family, friends, and perhaps some charities. However, more inventive gifts are also possible. If you wish, you can leave some money for friends to throw a party every year on your behalf, or to sponsor a series of jazz (or classical or western) concerts. An anonymous benefactor of the college I went to earned my life-long gratitude by endowing the milk supply in the dining hall, so all us milk lovers could always have as much as we wanted.

---

[2]To remind you, I use the word "gift" instead of the terms "bequest" and "devise" to mean any property passed under a will.

If you wish, you can also provide commentary on your gifts. For example[3]:

I give _$10,000_
to _my veterinarian, Dr. Surehands, for all her kind and competent treatment of my pets over the years_ or, if
Dr. Surehands does not
survive me by 45 days, to _____.

I give _my outboard motor_
to _my good friend, Hank Pike, who always enjoyed fishing with me on the lake_ or, if
Hank does not
survive me by 45 days, to _____.

Similarly, there are times, particularly in family situations, when an explanation of the reasons for your gifts is sensible. For example:

I give my residuary estate, i.e., the rest of my property not otherwise specifically and validly disposed of by this will or in any other manner, to _40% each to my son Charles and my daughter Dianne and 20% to my son Tim_ or if _they_ fail to survive me by 45 days, to _____. _I love all my children deeply and equally. I give 20% of the residue to Tim because he received family funds to go through medical school, so it is fair that my other two children receive more of my property now_.

A will can be a place for expressing your final sentiments, fond or not so fond. Short of libel[4], the scope of your remarks is limited only by your imagination. I know of wills in which the writers expressed at some length their love for a mate, children and friends.

By contrast, Benjamin Franklin's will left his son William, who was sympathetic to England during our Revolution, only some land in Nova Scotia, and stated, "The fact he acted against me in the late war, which is of public notoriety, will account for my leaving him no more of an estate that he endeavored to deprive me of." And then there was the German poet Heinrich Heine

---

[3]When we provide examples in this chapter, we employ the same format you will be using when you actually draft your will in Chapters 11 or 12. This format includes some predetermined language and underlined blank spaces where you enter information.

[4]If you libel someone in your will, your estate can be liable for damages. ▲ If you want to say something disparaging in your will, check it with a lawyer.

who wrote a will coldly leaving his property to his wife on the condition that she remarry, so that "there will be at least one man to regret my death." William Shakespeare cryptically left his wife his "second best bed," a bequest that has intrigued Shakespearean scholars for centuries.

If you decide you want to express some sentiments in your will, it is fine to do it in your own words, whenever it seems appropriate.

Note on Gifts to a Married Person: When you make a gift to someone who is married, the gift is that person's individual or separate property if you make the gift only in his or her name. For example: "I give my antique clock to Mary Kestor."

This means Mary would be entitled to keep the entire gift in the event of divorce (assuming the gift had been kept separate, i.e., not commingled with other shared marital property so that the gift could no longer be separately identified). If you want to emphasize this intent, you can say: "I give my antique clock to Mary Kestor as her separate property."

By contrast, if you wish to make a gift to a married couple, simply make it in both their names. For example: "I give my silver bowl to Edna and Fred Whitman." Again, you can provide emphasis by stating: "I give my silver bowl to Mr. and Mrs. Fred Whitman, as husband and wife."

Note on Forgiveness of Debts: One type of gift you can make in your will is to forgive a debt, i.e., release the person who owes you the debt from responsibility to pay it. Any debt, written or oral, can be forgiven. If you are married and forgiving a debt, be sure you have full power to do so. If the debt was incurred while you were married, you may only have the right to forgive half the debt (especially in community property states) unless your spouse agrees in writing to allow you to forgive his or her share of the debt as well. To forgive debts you will need to use Chapter 12 to draft your will rather than Chapter 11.

C. Restrictions on Gifts

There are only a very few legal restrictions on your power to leave property in your will. While these rarely apply, let's be extra cautious and review them briefly:

• Some felons, and anyone who unlawfully caused the death of the person who wrote the will, cannot be inheritors;

• You cannot attempt to encourage or restrain some types of conduct of your beneficiaries. For example, you cannot make a gift contingent on the marriage, divorce, or change of religion of a recipient;

• You cannot validly leave money for an illegal purpose, e.g., to establish the Institute for the Encouragement of Drug Addiction.

▲ In addition to these legal prohibitions on gifts, the Will Book further limits the types of gifts you can make. Specifically, complex shared gifts (discussed in Section F below) and gifts of a "life estate" or trusts, where a beneficiary only gets the use of the property during his or her life (discussed in Section K), cannot be made by the use of the Will Book. This is because I believe that for each of these types of gifts, the help of an attorney is essential.

Also, you cannot make a conditional gift using the Will Book. For example, you cannot leave money to a nephew, Ed, if he goes to veterinary school, but, if he does not, to your niece Polly. The reason for this is that I believe most conditional gifts create far more problems than they solve. To continue the example of Ed, the potential animal doctor, here are just a few problems inherent in this approach: How soon must Ed go to veterinary school? What happens if he applies in good faith but fails to get in? Who decides if he's really studying? What happens to the money before Ed goes to veterinary school?

▲ In any situation where you want to impose conditions on a gift, someone must be responsible for being sure the conditions are fulfilled. The best way to do this is by leaving the property in a trust to be managed by a trustee. Aside from property left to your children in a simple trust designed to delay the age at which they inherit property to an age older than eighteen (see Chapter 7), you cannot impose these types of controls on property by using the Will Book. Unfortunately, the types of trusts necessary to exercise such control are not available in a self-help law format, and require the assistance of a lawyer.

D. Divorce

As previously mentioned, in several states a final judgment of divorce (or annulment) does not automatically revoke any gift made by your will to your former spouse. In a few others, it may revoke the entire will. Therefore, after a divorce you should revoke your old will[5] and make a new one. It is not necessary to specifically disinherit a former spouse; simply leaving this person out of your will achieves the same result. Of course, if you want to emphasize your feelings, you can specifically state in your new will that your former spouse is to receive nothing from your estate.

E. Disinheritance

Except as restricted by marital property laws, which in all non-community property states allow a spouse to demand at least a portion of your estate, you can disinherit anyone you want to. If you decide, however, to disinherit a child, or grandchild if that child's parent (i.e., your child) has predeceased you,[6] you must do so expressly by specifically declaring your intention in your will (e.g., "I disinherit my son, Nero, and declare he shall receive nothing from my estate"). In other words, unlike the situation with all other people, merely leaving a child (or child of a deceased child) out of your will does not "disinherit" that child (see Chapter 7, Section D). Again, anyone else can be disinherited simply by omitting to name him or her as a beneficiary.

Note: If you want to disinherit a child or child of a deceased child, you must prepare your will from Chapter 12 rather than use one of the Chapter 11 form wills. Or put another way, use a Chapter 11 will only if you plan to leave at least some property to all your children and the children of any of your deceased children.

You may have heard that some lawyers recommend leaving $1 to relatives you want to disinherit. Is doing this legally necessary? No. There is generally no need to mention a relative, or anyone else, in your will only to leave them one dollar. If, however, you think a relative might try to contest your will, you might leave that relative $1, to make it absolutely clear you did consider her and wanted to give no more. This same approach may be used if you do not wish to provide substantially for a child (or child of a deceased child) but do not want to disinherit him or her explicitly. This issue is specifically addressed in Chapter 7.

F. Shared Gifts

If you leave all your property in a series of gifts, each designated to go to one person or organ-ization, you do not need to worry about the troubling questions that can arise in making a shared gift and should skip this section and go on to Section G of this chapter. Because of the difficulties shared gifts can create, the Will Book recommends that you avoid making them, if possible. But what if you really do wish to leave your antique music box, or your wonderful '55 T-Bird converti-

---

[5]This is easily and routinely done by a sentence in the new will.

[6]You can disinherit all your grandchildren with parents (i.e., your children) who are alive simply by omitting those grandchildren from your will.

ble or your one major asset, your house, to all three of your children? Let's look at the problems you face when you leave one piece of property to more than one person.

1. Percentage of Ownership

The first question that arises with shared gifts is what percentage of ownership each beneficiary gets. If you want the gift shared equally, simply say so:

I give the property commonly known as _1123 Elm St., Centerville (my house)_
to _my three children, Anne, Rob and Tony in equal shares_ or, if _they_ do not
survive me by 45 days, to _my brother Fred_.

If you don't specify the shares, it is presumed that you intended equal shares. You can, of course, divide ownership up in any way you decide:

I give the property commonly known as _111 11th St. (my house) and all furniture, rugs, appliances and household goods_
to _40% to my spouse Mary, 20% to my son John, 20% to my daughter Mildred, and 20% to my brother Tim_ or, if _they_ do not
survive me by 45 days, to _The Wildlife Foundation_.

If you do this, make sure your numbers add up to 100%.

2. Control

Control is the most basic problem with shared ownership. Suppose the people you've given a gift to disagree about how to use it. To return to the example of the house given to the three children, suppose two want to sell it, and another doesn't. Who prevails?

You can put provisions in your will governing this, e.g., "The house cannot be sold unless all three of my children agree on it." But often other problems follow. If two want to sell the house, but one doesn't, who has to manage the house? Does the house have to be rented at market value? Can the child who wants to keep the house live in it? If she does, must she pay the others any rent? What happens if one child dies? The difficulties of dealing with these types of complications is why I recommend against getting into specifying details of long-term control of property you leave your beneficiaries.

However, in some situations you may be confident your clause covers any problems which can arise. For example, this sort of clause probably does not really need a lawyer's review:

I give ___my antique music box___

to ___my three children to share equally. It may not be sold unless all three agree on that sale. (sharing the music box means each child shall retain possession of the music box for four months during each calendar year)___ or, if ___any of them___ do not survive me by 45 days, to _____.

If a shared gift is to be divided immediately after your death, problems of control must be resolved promptly. If you think your beneficiaries will agree on division of the property, there's no problem. For example, this sort of clause should cause no difficulties if the beneficiaries cooperate.

I give ___all my household furnishings and possessions equally___

to ___my children Mike and Spike___ or, if ___they___ do not survive me by 45 days, to _____.

However, if you're worried about conflict, you can appoint someone to resolve any which arise:

I give ___all my household furnishings and possessions equally___

to ___my children Mike and Spike, to be divided by them, or if they cannot agree, the equal division shall be made by my executor___ or, if ___they___ do not survive me by 45 days, to _____.

Another way to deal with this situation is to discuss it with the proposed beneficiaries. If there's genuine agreement between them, potential problems are less likely to become real ones. If you conclude there's genuinely no risk of conflict, you can simply make the shared gift without any conditions or directions, leaving it entirely up to the beneficiaries to resolve any problems.

If you don't spell out in your will how these questions are to be resolved (for example, by the executor), and if the beneficiaries can't agree, the courts will decide for you. For example, if co-owners disagree about selling a house, any of them has the right to obtain a court order directing that the house be sold and the proceeds divided among the co-owners.

▲ In general, you should have any clauses you draft concerning controls over a shared gift reviewed by a lawyer. A lawyer can also tell you the rule that governs shared ownership in the absence of instructions in your will.

G. Naming an Alternate Beneficiary

What happens if a person (or persons) named in your will to receive a gift fails to survive you? Who gets the property? More to the point, should you address this contingency in your will? The answer to this last question is a definite "yes." No matter how simple your plan regarding your property, you should routinely provide for the possibility that each person you name as a bene - ficiary may fail to survive you.

Your first thought may be that this isn't necessary because you can simply write a new will if a named beneficiary dies before you. Most of the time you can and should. But what if you are incapacitated when this occurs, or you die very soon after the named beneficiary, or you just don't get around to it? Enough said, I hope.

If you don't name an alternate beneficiary for a gift, all wills prepared from the Will Book pro - vide that if the primary beneficiary fails to survive you by the period indicated in the will,[7] the gift becomes part of the residue and goes to your residuary beneficiary. Thus, if your residuary beneficiary is the same person you want to receive a particular gift if a specifically-named bene -

---

[7] All wills in Chapter 11 provide for a survivorship period of 45 days. The reason why this survivorship period is chosen is discussed in Section I of this chapter. If you are using Chapter 12 to make your will, you can set this survivorship period yourself.

ficiary dies, it's not strictly necessary that you name an alternate for that gift, because your will has already done that.

Example: Betsy McCray leaves a gift of $10,000 to her friend Daniel Carlan. Her will names her two children, Kendell McCray and Sara Peters, as her residuary beneficiaries. Betsy does not name any specific alternate beneficiary because she wants Kendell and Sara to have the property, if Daniel fails to survive her by 45 days. If this occurs, the $10,000 gift becomes part of the residue, to be divided between Kendell and Sara, which is what Betsy wants. Sara would enter this information in the Beneficiary Chart in this chapter as follows:

___*$10,000*___ to ___*Daniel Carlan*___
Amount   Beneficiary

___(left blank)___
Alternate Beneficiary

Assuming you do not want your residuary beneficiary to inherit all of your property (should all of the people you have named to inherit a gift fail to survive you by the period specified in your will), this book offers you the opportunity to name an alternate beneficiary for each gift. There are different considerations for naming an alternate beneficiary to receive a shared gift than when you name a single beneficiary. Because the overwhelming number of readers will prefer to follow my advice and make each gift to a single individual, I will first tell you how to handle this. Then, in subsection 2 below, I will show you how the wills in this book help you handle alternate beneficiaries for shared gifts.

1. Alternate Beneficiaries for Individual Gifts

To name an alternate beneficiary for a gift to an individual, simply enter that person's or organization's name on the appropriate line in the worksheet in this chapter. Then, when you make your will using either the Chapter 11 or Chapter 12 approach, you will follow instructions and transfer this information to the appropriate will clause. Please reassure yourself by turning over a few pages and taking a look at how simple the worksheet really is that none of this is particularly difficult.

Example 1: Sal Benito decides to leave her antique piano to her brother Tim Jones. In case Tim fails to survive her by 45 days, Sal wants her sister Ruth Jones as alternate beneficiary. At this point, she simply enters this information in the appropriate box on the Beneficiary Chart as follows:

___*my antique piano*___
Item

to ___*Tim Jones*___
Beneficiary(ies)

___*Ruth Jones*___
Alternate Beneficiary(ies)

There is no rule regarding who you should name as alternates for gifts made to individuals; that's up to you. For example, many people will divide the bulk of their property among their children. As an alternate beneficiary for each particular piece of property left to one child should that child fail to survive them by the period specified in the will, these people will name their other child (or children). Others will prefer to deal with this same possibility by designating the children of the deceased child (their grandchildren), or a friend as alternate beneficiaries.

Example 2: Sal Benito prepares a will leaving her house to her son Peter Benito. In case Peter does not survive her by 45 days, Sal names her other child, Peggy Abrams, as alternate beneficiary. She would do this on the Beneficiary Chart as follows:

my house at 11 Garden Lane, Boston
Property Address

to _Peter Benito_
Beneficiary(ies)

Peggy Abrams
Alternate Beneficiary(ies)

If possible, I advise naming just one person or institution as alternate beneficiary for each gift. If, however, you really do want the gift to go to more than one person should the primary bene - ficiary fail to survive you by the period specified in the will, you can accomplish this by naming both or all of them. It's best to do this by naming each person individually rather than using a general term such as "all my other children." However, if your child Mary, a beneficiary, has one child and may have more, you can name as alternate beneficiaries (should Mary fail to survive you) "her children, in equal shares."

Example 3: Sal Jones' will leaves her summer home to Ruth Abrams. If Ruth does not survive her by 45 days, Sal's will provides that the alternate beneficiaries are "Ruth Abram's children, in equal shares." She would accomplish this on the Beneficiary Chart as follows:

my summer home at Old Forge Pond, New York
Property Address

to _Ruth Abrams_
Beneficiary(ies)

Ruth Abrams' children in equal shares
Alternate Beneficiary(ies)

▲ All this seems simple enough, and it usually is. However, if you want to move to the next level of contingencies, it can get complicated. To continue with Example 3, suppose Sal wants to consider what happens if both Ruth and one of Ruth's children fail to survive her by the required period. Or Sal wants to impose controls over the gift if Ruth's children receive it because Ruth has failed to survive her. Handling these types of remote contingencies is tricky, and if you want to get in this deep, you'll need to see a lawyer. However, frankly, I think a more sensible way to handle these types of unlikely-to-occur contingencies is to keep your will up to date.

2. Alternate Beneficiaries for Shared Gifts

When it comes to shared gifts, providing an alternate beneficiary is more complicated. The reason is that more than one possibility must be provided for. The best way to appreciate this is to suppose that you leave your house in equal shares to A, B, and C. What happens if B dies? Does the house go equally to A and C, or equally to A, C, and B's children, or does B's share go to another named alternate beneficiary or the residuary beneficiary? And, if this isn't enough complexity for you to think about, consider the question of what happens if A and B, or even A, B and C all fail to survive you by the period specified in the will.

Clearly, a little order is needed so you don't give up and run to a lawyer. The Will Book provides this order by simplifying your choices. In all shared gift situations, the wills in this book state that if one of the named beneficiaries dies before you do, the other or others divide(s) that person's share. Thus, to return to the example above, if you make a gift to A, B and C, and B predeceases you, A and C share the entire gift. Only if A, B and C all fail to survive you by the period specified in the will does an alternate named by you in your will take the gift.

Example: Ethel Turk is a widow with three children, Maude, Patricia and Elliot. Ethel leaves her house to all three in equal shares. She names her close friend Mary Rogers as alternate beneficiary. If Maude fails to survive Ethel by the period specified in the will, and Ethel does not change her will, Patricia and Elliot will jointly inherit the house and Mary Rogers will inherit nothing. Mary will only get the house if Maude, Elliot and Patricia fail to survive Ethel by the requisite period and Ethel does not change that provision in her will.

▲ As mentioned above, while the method I provide should meet most people's needs, there are other ways to take care of shared gifts should one of the group of named beneficiaries predecease you. Many of these are quite complicated and are outside the scope of this book. See a lawyer if you need to write a provision for alternate beneficiaries for shared gifts.

H. Beneficiary Chart

Okay, it's time to start to pin down who will receive your property. In the following chart you'll list your property, using descriptions from the chart in Chapter 5.[8] First identify each item of your property you want to give as a distinct gift. Select only from the property items that you have designated with a "W" in the box in the left margin. Then list a beneficiary or beneficiaries for each item. Use full names and provide extra identification if the names are extremely common or there may otherwise be confusion as to who you mean. You don't normally need to list addresses unless you think the beneficiary might be hard for your executor to find. If you give one item of property to be shared by more than one beneficiary, be sure you have considered the concerns discussed in Section 5. After naming your primary beneficiary or beneficiaries, you will want to put down your choice for an alternate, as outlined in Section G above.

After you go through the first four sections of the Beneficiary Chart and make all specific gifts of personal and real property, name alternate beneficiaries and forgive debts (if desired), you'll use Section 5 to name your residuary beneficiary. This person, or persons, receives all property that you haven't otherwise given away in your will. Some people choose to make only a few specific gifts—heirlooms or cash gifts, for example—and leave the bulk of their estate to spouses or children through a residuary clause. More typically, people will make a number of specific gifts and name a residuary beneficiary to take what is left over.

Before you name a residuary beneficiary, keep in mind that:

---

[8]Of course, if you didn't use this chart because of the simplicity of your desires or property situation, there is no need to return to that chapter.

1. The residue of your estate may contain a great deal of property. Everything you own at your death that is not otherwise given away is included in the residue. That includes property you overlook when you make your will, or that you acquire later, or that for some reason cannot go to the persons you specifically willed it to. Also, the value of the residue can increase substantially if the value of residual property (stock or land, for example) goes up.

2. The residue is commonly the first thing to be used to pay for your taxes, debts, and specific monetary gifts if you haven't specified an adequate source of funds to accomplish this. In addition, while the rule varies from state to state, in most states, any shortfalls in specific gifts of money are made up first from the residue, unless you state in the will a different preference. The same may be true if a spouse is eligible to take against the will and decides to do so (see Chapter 4, Section F).

Note: Chapter 12 contains clauses that allow you to specify that you want any shortfalls in money to be dealt with in other ways.

Okay, now it's time to fill in the chart. To do so, follow these steps:

Step 1: Make your cash gifts, specifying the amount, the names of the primary beneficiaries, and the names of the alternate beneficiaries. Make sure the total amount of your cash gifts is in line with the total value of your liquid assets (e.g., bank accounts, bonds, stocks, etc) as described in the Chapter 5 property inventory chart.

Step 2: Turn back to the property chart you prepared in Chapter 5.

Step 3: Transfer each item (or category of items) that you want to make a specific gift of from that chart to this chart according to its item # and a brief shorthand description.

Example: Under item #10 on the Chapter 5 property chart, Tom Jones describes his car as follows: "1968 Mustang Convertible, Red, I.D. # D23769523, Lic. # 1DSF234." Tom transfers that item to this chart as follows: "#10-Mustang."

Step 4: Name primary beneficiary or beneficiaries.

Step 5: Name alternate beneficiary or beneficiaries.

Step 6: If you wish to forgive debts, enter the appropriate information in Part 3 of the chart.

Beneficiary Chart

1. Specific Cash Bequests

_____ to _____
Amount   Beneficiary

_____
Alternate Beneficiary

_____ to _____
Amount   Beneficiary

_____
Alternate Beneficiary

_____ to _____
Amount   Beneficiary

_____
Alternate Beneficiary

_____ to _____
Amount   Beneficiary

_____
Alternate Beneficiary

_____ to _____
Amount   Beneficiary

_____
Alternate Beneficiary

_____ to _____
Amount   Beneficiary

_____
Alternate Beneficiary

_____ to _____
Amount   Beneficiary

_____
Alternate Beneficiary

_____ to _____
Amount   Beneficiary

_____
Alternate Beneficiary

_____ to _____
Amount   Beneficiary

_____
Alternate Beneficiary

_____ to _____
Amount   Beneficiary

_____
Alternate Beneficiary

2. Gifts of Specific Personal Property

Item _____

to _____
   Beneficiary(ies)

_____
Alternate Beneficiary(ies)

Item _____

to _____
   Beneficiary(ies)

_____
Alternate Beneficiary(ies)

Item _____

to _____
   Beneficiary(ies)

_____
Alternate Beneficiary(ies)

Item _____

to _____
   Beneficiary(ies)

_____
Alternate Beneficiary(ies)

Item _____

to _____
   Beneficiary(ies)

_____
Alternate Beneficiary(ies)

Item _____

to _____
   Beneficiary(ies)

_____
Alternate Beneficiary(ies)

Item _____

to _____
   Beneficiary(ies)

_____
Alternate Beneficiary(ies)

Item _____

to _____
Beneficiary(ies)

Alternate Beneficiary(ies)

Item _____

to _____
Beneficiary(ies)

Alternate Beneficiary(ies)

Item _____

to _____
Beneficiary(ies)

Alternate Beneficiary(ies)

Item _____

to _____
Beneficiary(ies)

Alternate Beneficiary(ies)

Item _____

to _____
Beneficiary(ies)

Alternate Beneficiary(ies)

Item _____

to _____
Beneficiary(ies)

Alternate Beneficiary(ies)

Item _____

to _____
Beneficiary(ies)

Alternate Beneficiary(ies)

3. Debts Forgiven

_____ to _____
Amount Forgiven   Debtor

_____
Date of Loan

_____ to _____
Amount Forgiven   Debtor

_____
Date of Loan

_____ to _____
Amount Forgiven   Debtor

_____
Date of Loan

_____ to _____
Amount Forgiven   Debtor

_____
Date of Loan

_____ to _____
Amount Forgiven   Debtor

_____
Date of Loan

4. Gifts of Real Estate

_____
Property Address

to _____
     Beneficiary(ies)

_____
Alternate Beneficiary(ies)

_____
Property Address

to _____
     Beneficiary(ies)

_____
Alternate Beneficiary(ies)

_____
Property Address

to _____
     Beneficiary(ies)

_____
Alternate Beneficiary(ies)

Property Address
_____

to _____
Beneficiary(ies)

_____
Alternate Beneficiary(ies)

Property Address
_____

to _____
Beneficiary(ies)

_____
Alternate Beneficiary(ies)

Property Address
_____

to _____
Beneficiary(ies)

_____
Alternate Beneficiary(ies)

Property Address
_____

to _____
Beneficiary(ies)

_____
Alternate Beneficiary(ies)

5. Residuary Beneficiary or Beneficiaries (to receive the rest of your estate after all specific gifts are made)

Note: It's particularly important to name an alternate beneficiary for your residue, since this may constitute the bulk of your property. In case your residuary beneficiary predeceases you, you want to be sure you've specified where this property goes. There's no fall-back option built into your will here, as there is for specific gifts (which become part of your residue as a last resort).

If you name more than one person, or one organization, to share your residue, here is what happens (under all of the wills in this book) if one of these people does not survive you by the number of days provided in your will. The surviving named beneficiaries of the shared residue will take the deceased beneficiary's share. In other words, in a shared residue situation, the alternate beneficiary you name will only inherit if all of the people you name to share the residue of your estate fail to survive you by the period specified in your will. This is exactly the same plan as discussed in Section G(2) above and illustrated in the example of Ethel Turk and her three children. Enter your choices for residuary and alternate residuary beneficiaries in the spaces below.

_____
Residuary Beneficiary's Name

_____
Alternate Residuary Beneficiary

After completing the beneficiary chart, read further in this chapter if you want to know more about:

• Why survivorship periods are a good idea (Section I);

• What happens if you and your spouse die simultaneously (Section J);

• Leaving property to someone for use during his or her life only (called a "life estate") and then having it pass to someone else (Section K);

• Property left in a will that you don't own at death (Section L); or

• What happens if you don't have enough liquid assets to pay each gift (Section M).

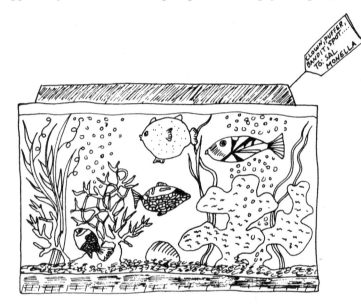

I. Establishing a Survivorship Period

A survivorship period means that a beneficiary, or an alternate beneficiary, must survive the will writer by a specified time period to inherit. One reason for imposing survivorship periods on gifts is to avoid double death taxes and probate costs. If the person to whom you leave property dies soon after you, the property will be included in his estate. The result is that the property you'd hoped the person would use and enjoy merely raises the dollar value of his estate, possibly increasing its taxes and becoming subject to additional probate fees. Also, this property now passes under the terms of your beneficiary's will, rather than being given to someone you've chosen. To avoid all this, most wills set a specific time period by which a beneficiary must survive the will writer.

Example: "I give my 1955 T-Bird to my best friend Anthony, or, if he does not survive me by 45 days, to my cousin Jacques de Paris."

▲ All basic wills in Chapter 11 have a 45-day survivorship period for your primary benefici - aries. In a Chapter 12 will you have the opportunity to select any reasonable survivorship period you want (or none at all) to apply to all primary beneficiaries. My preference is for relatively short periods, 45 to 60 days, to be sure you haven't tied property up beyond the time practically required to transfer it. If no probate is required, as is often the case for small estates and gifts made to a surviving spouse, property can be transferred to beneficiaries in a matter of days or weeks. But since formal probate often takes at least six months (and sometimes more than one year), there are also sensible arguments for a lengthier survivorship period, say 180 days. If you want to choose a period longer than this, see a lawyer.

J. Simultaneous Death

Many couples, married or not, who will their property to each other wonder what would hap-pen to the property if they were to die in the same accident or occurrence. The usual answer is simple. Assuming a survivorship clause is used (See Section I above), the property left to the other spouse or mate as a primary beneficiary will pass to the alternate beneficiary. If, however, either or both of you leave property to the other and there is no survivorship clause in operation, or there is no alternate beneficiary, what happens?

In the absence of a special clause (called a simultaneous death clause), your property may pass to your spouse (or mate) or vice versa. This means that your spouse's heirs will receive your property or your heirs will receive your spouse's property. Hardly the result that either of you would intend.

To prevent this from happening I recommend the use in a will of a "simultaneous death" clause, providing that when it is difficult to tell who died first, and no survivorship clause covers the gift, the property of each person is disposed of as if he survived the other.

You may ask, "How logically can a simultaneous death provision work? How can I be presumed to have outlived my spouse for purposes of my will, but then she's presumed to have outlived me for purposes of her will?" The answer to this paradox is that, under the law, each of your wills will be interpreted independently of the other. Thus, each provision in your separate wills provides the result each of you would most likely intend.

Example: Martha and George, a married couple, die in a plane wreck. Both their wills have simultaneous death provisions. Thus George's property, which he willed entirely to Martha, does not go to her because under the simultaneous death clause, Martha is presumed to have already been dead when George died. George's property goes to whomever he named as alternate or residu-ary beneficiary. This same process is repeated for Martha's property; it goes not to George but to the alternate beneficiaries.

You'll find a simultaneous death clause in the basic wills for a married couple and for a person living with a lover/mate. It is also included in the "assemble-a-will" approach in Chapter 12.

What happens if people (spouses or otherwise) who own joint tenancy property die simultan-eously? The property is divided into as many equal shares as there are joint tenants. Then a share is given to each owner's estate.

Example: Jim and Mary Smith, owners of a house in joint tenancy, die together in a plane crash. One half of the joint tenancy property is included in Jim Smith's estate. The other half is included in Mary Smith's estate.

Under the wills prepared from the Will Book, your share of any joint tenancy property which becomes part of your estate because of simultaneous death of you and the other joint owners becomes part of your residue, unless you make other express provision for that share. An example of this express provision would be:

I give _any joint tenancy property which becomes part of my estate_

to _Mary Jones_ or, if

Mary Jones does not

survive me by 45 days, to _Tim Jones_ .

Remember, though, that if one joint tenant does survive the other(s), that tenant receives all the joint tenancy property, no matter what your will says.

K. Life Estates

As previously mentioned, the Will Book does not show you how to create what's called a "life estate." This is property left for the use of one beneficiary for his or her life, which then passes to another beneficiary when the life beneficiary dies. However, because life estates can be important to some people's estate planning needs, let's take a closer look at how they work.

Example: Marilyn James is married to Martin Smith. Marilyn has two grown children from her first marriage. Marilyn's major asset is the house she owns, which she and Martin have lived in for ten years. In Marilyn's will she leaves the house to Martin in a life estate. This means Martin has the right to use of the house during his lifetime, but upon his death the life estate terminates and the house goes to Marilyn's children.

▲ The usual way to create a life estate is by a trust. In the above example, Marilyn would need a life estate trust as part of her will to accomplish her desires. Drafting this type of trust requires the assistance of a lawyer. It may seem simple at first, but it is not. For example, here are only a few of the questions that can arise:

• Does the surviving spouse, the one with the "life estate" interest, have the right to sell the house and buy another one?

• Suppose the surviving spouse has massive medical bills. Can he encumber the house to get money to pay the bills?

• Can he rent the house?

• What right do the wife's children have to find out what the husband is doing regarding the house?

All these problems, and more, should be resolved in the language establishing the trust. There are also technical IRS requirements which must be met, and a mistake in complying with these can be disastrous in tax terms. Further, since a trust cannot be changed or amended once the will writer dies and may last for many years, a poorly drafted trust can cause all sorts of problems down the road.

If you do decide you want to see a lawyer to establish a life estate trust, don't just turn the whole matter over to him or her. Carefully sketch out the substance of what you want (and the contingencies you are worried about), before you see the lawyer.

L. Property You Leave In Your Will That You No Longer Own at Your Death

A will is not binding until the death of the will writer. Before then, you can give away or sell any property mentioned in your will. Even if the will is never amended or re-written to recognize that you no longer own particular pieces of property, the gift or sale is valid.

But what happens when you do dispose of property and cause a discrepancy between what your will provides and the amount or type of property actually left in your estate when you die? Or putting the same question somewhat differently, what happens if at your death your will leaves people more or different property than is actually available for distribution?

If you've given someone a specific piece of property in your will (say a particular Tiffany lamp) but you no longer own that property when you die, that beneficiary is out of luck. Lawyers all this "ademption." People who don't inherit the property in question are often heard to use an earthier term.

M. When You Have Insufficient Liquid Assets To Pay Your Cash Gifts

A similar problem to the one discussed above occurs when there isn't enough money to go around. You might simply spend some of the money you left people in your will. In addition, your debts, taxes, funeral expenses, and probate fees must be paid before your cash gifts can be made and if all these expenses reduce your estate to less than the amount your cash gifts add up to someone is obviously out of luck. One cause for depletion of the cash in an estate occurs if a resident of a common law state leaves her spouse such a small portion of her estate that the spouse is able to "take against the will" (See Chapter 4 Section F). Another cause is when a willmaker fails to either mention or provide for one of his children in his will, thus qualifying the child as an "overlooked" heir who is entitled to a share of the willmaker's estate, under law (see Chapter 7).

If your will disposes of more than you have, this necessitates what is called an "abatement" in legalese. "Abatement" works as follows. Absent a specific directive by the will writer (that's you) in the will, the law of each state provides the rules for how the executor of an estate must conduct abatement proceedings. Some states require that property first be taken from the residue and sold; others first require a pro-rata reduction of cash gifts, if possible without the sale of specific objects of property. If property must be sold, unspecified property (i.e., property from your estate's residue) is generally the first to be used, then specific gifts of personal property, then specific gifts of real estate. The details of how different states reduce gifts vary too much to be covered here.

The wills in Chapter 11 allow abatement to be carried out according to the laws of each state. Chapter 12, on the other hand, contains two different abatement clauses. One provides that short - falls in specific cash gifts are to be made up from the residue.[9] The other provides for pro-rata reduction of all cash gifts if there isn't enough money to pay them in full. If you choose the residue option, and there is a shortage of cash available to pay all cash gifts, the people who receive your residue will lose out first. If the residue is still not sufficient to account for a cash deficit in your estate, the executor is directed to abate in the most equitable (fair) way possible consistent with state law.

Example if Residuary Option Is Chosen: Paul leaves $20,000 to Steve, Stephanie, Barbara and Jack. When he dies there is only $40,000 in cash in his estate. However, Paul's estate also con - tains a house for which he has named no beneficiary. To pay the full amount of the cash gifts, the house must be sold. The residuary beneficiary takes what is left over after the cash gifts are paid.

Example if Pro-Rata Option Is Chosen: If you pick the pro-rata reduction clause and there is not enough money to pay for the cash gifts, all cash gifts will be reduced by the same percentage. This percentage is determined by dividing the total amount of cash originally given in the will into the total amount actually available for making gifts.

Example: Robert makes cash bequests of $20,000 to Kate, John, Mary, and Toni. When he dies there is only $40,000 in his estate after debts and burial expenses are paid. The four benefi - ciaries receive $10,000 each.

If you don't include either clause, any necessary abatement will be conducted in accordance with your state's statutes.

▲ **Warning:** The subject of what happens if you leave more property in your will than is actually available is far too complex to cover here in any meaningful detail. However, the overall point is simple. Don't give away more than you own, after what you owe and what your estate will need to pay in tax is subtracted. Make a new will whenever your property situation changes significantly. If you desire more information about how your property will be distributed in the event an abatement (reduction of gifts) is required (i.e., your estate comes up short), consult an attorney knowledgeable in such matters.

---

[9]The residue, remember, is all of your property which has not been specifically described and given to someone by your will.

CHAPTER 7:

Children

This chapter need only be read if you are concerned with children. Sections A, B, and C discuss issues for those who have minor children. Section D covers the rules for disinheriting a child or grandchild. Section E reviews questions concerning adopted children and briefly discusses the inheritance rights of "illegitimate" children. Finally, Section F is designed for anyone who wants to leave property to a minor child other than his own. As you proceed through this chapter, you'll make and enter choices regarding your will and (your) children, so keep your pencil, and your wits, handy.

A. Custody of Your Minor Children After Your Death

A serious worry for parents with minor children is what will happen to the children in the event the parents die. Indeed, creating a legal, and personally chosen, method for handling this grim possibility is the major goal many younger parents want to achieve by their wills. Many parents of minors ask questions like:

- "What happens to our children if we're both killed simultaneously?"

- "My ex-husband has disappeared for years. Could he get custody if I die?"

- "I have custody of the kids and I've remarried. My present wife is, and would be, a much better mother to my daughter than my ex-wife, who never cared for her properly. What can I do to make sure my wife gets custody if I die?"

- "I'm a single mother. My son is almost sixteen and very responsible. Can I leave my property directly to him?"

The starting point for answering most questions regarding wills and minors is the law that a minor child must have an adult guardian unless he is legally "emancipated." The determination of who is a "minor" is a matter of state law. Most states declare that anyone under age 18 is a minor, while a few specify age 19 or 21.[1]

The first rule regarding custody of children is that children are not property. You cannot will them to whoever you want to have custody. If there are two parents willing and able to care for the children, and one dies, the other generally takes over physical custody. With a continuing marriage, this presents no problem.

But what if the parents are divorced, and one has primary custody while the other has visitation rights? Usually, if the custodial parent dies, the surviving parent will legally gain custody. But this is not invariably true. If a parent has legally "abandoned"[2] a child, a court may award custody to someone else. Also, if it's demonstrated in a court proceeding that a surviving parent is "unfit," custody can be granted to another person. It should be noted, however, that it is usually quite difficult to prove that a parent is unfit unless he or she has serious problems such as alcohol abuse or mental problems, etc. The fact that you don't like or respect the other parent is never enough.

But what happens if both parents die simultaneously? Or what if the parent with custody believes the other natural parent is incapable of properly caring for the children or simply won't assume the responsibility? Or suppose the custodial parent has remarried, and believes, with good reason, that the children's stepparent would be the best guardian and that the other parent isn't a fit parent? Or what is to be done if the other natural parent is deceased, or vanished, or otherwise out of the picture? The answer to all these questions is—it's not certain what will happen.

Whenever there is no surviving parent willing to assume custody, or that parent's fitness to do so is seriously challenged, a court will make the final decision as to who will be guardian. How - ever, and this is the important point, this judicial decision can be heavily influenced by your choice for guardian, if you make one in your will. Although not binding on the court, your nomination will generally be followed unless there is a surviving parent who claims custody and who is judged fit to care for the child. Therefore it can be helpful to spell out either in your will or in an attachment to it why you believe the person named as guardian can best care for your children.

Example 1: Liz, the custodial parent of Amanda, has remarried Brad, who has raised Liz's child with her since the child was a year old. Amanda's father (Liz's ex) has no interest in Amanda and has not taken care of her for years. So Liz specifies in her will that if she dies, she wants Brad to be appointed guardian of Amanda. She includes a paragraph giving the date Brad began caring for Amanda, describing how he's functioned as a parent, and that Amanda's father hasn't taken any interest in the child, nor paid any child support for six years.

---

[1] An "emancipated minor" refers to a person under the legal age for adulthood who has nevertheless achieved legal adult status. The rules for emancipation are governed by your state's laws; normal grounds are marriage, military service, or factual independence validated by court order. Emancipation is uncommon. Most importantly, for this book's purposes, you cannot emancipate your child through your will.

[2] "Abandonment" must be declared in a judicial proceeding, where a court finds that a parent has substantially failed to contact or support a child for an extended period of time, usually at least a year or two. A parent who has legally abandoned a child loses many of her normal parental rights over that child.

If Liz dies, this statement in the will can be very helpful for Brad. Unlike a natural or adoptive parent, a stepparent[3] is not legally presumed to be the best guardian for a child. However, unless Amanda's natural father contests Liz's specification of Brad as guardian, it will probably be honored. And even if the natural father does seek custody, it will not automatically be granted to him. Brad can file a custody suit, asserting that the ex-husband legally "abandoned" his child, and use Liz's will as evidence that granting him custody will be in Amanda's best interest.

Now, let's explore some basic child custody principles through a series of examples.

• Parents should agree on who they want appointed guardian of their minor children.

Example: Ariadne uses her will to name her sister, Penny, to serve as personal guardian in the event that her husband, Ralph, dies at the same time as she does or is otherwise unavailable to care for the children. As it turns out, Ralph and Ariadne die in a plane crash. Ralph's mother wants custody of the children, but the court appoints Penny, since no evidence has been introduced which would prevent her from serving as the children's legal guardian. If Ralph's will had named his mother as guardian, however, then the court would have to choose between Penny and Ralph's mother. The lesson of this is clearly that Ralph and Ariadne should discuss this important issue and name the same person as guardian in their wills, if possible.

---

[3]Brad could become Amanda's legal father by a stepparent adoption, which could be routinely accomplished if her biological father were willing to relinquish his parental rights. This can be done in California without a lawyer by using *Adopt Your Stepchild* by Frank Zagone (Nolo Press).

• Natural parents have priority over others named as guardian in a will.

Example: Susan and Fred, an unmarried couple, have two minor children. Although Susan loves Fred, she doesn't think he is capable of raising the children on his own. She uses her will to name her mother, Elinor, as the children's personal guardian. If Susan dies, Fred, as the children's natural parent, will probably be given first priority over Elinor if the court finds he is willing and able to care for the children. If, however, the court finds it is not in the children's best interest to have Fred as their guardian,[4] Elinor would get the nod, assuming she was fit. Also, if Fred was not the natural father, but only the stepfather, Elinor would probably be named as the guardian if Susan had named her in the will.

• Courts usually follow the deceased parent's wishes as to the guardian, unless this choice conflicts with the rights of a natural parent.

Example: Now let's change a few facts and assume that Susan and Fred live together with Susan's minor children from an earlier marriage or relationship. The natural father is out of the picture, but Susan fears that her mother, Elinor, will try and get custody of the kids if something happens to her, partially because Elinor doesn't approve of anyone who "lives in sin." Susan wants Fred to have custody because he knows the children well and loves them, and uses her will to name Fred as personal guardian. Should something happen to Susan, and Elinor goes to court to try and get custody, the fact that Susan named Fred will give him a big advantage, especially if Susan had described in her will why Fred had been and would continue to be a good guardian. And, if he is in fact a good candidate for guardian, he will probably prevail in the great majority of states.[5]

• It is sometimes desirable to name different guardians for different children.

Example: Melissa has a 15-year-old daughter, Irene, from a first marriage, and two-year-old twins from her second marriage to Alfonso. Irene's father abandoned her years ago. Irene does not get along well with Alfonso. Melissa uses her will to name her friend Nancy to be Irene's guardian should something happen to her. As the twins' father, Alfonso would have custody of them if Melissa dies. If Melissa and Alfonso die simultaneously, they both name another friend to be guardian of the twins, because Nancy doesn't want that responsibility.

B. Name the Personal Guardian for Your Minor Children

Okay, enough background. In the space below, record your choice(s) for guardians of your children. You should also name a successor guardian in case your original choice can't serve. Later on, in Chapter 11 or Chapter 12, you will be inserting this choice into your will draft.

Remember the obvious: you can't draft someone to do the job. So be sure any person you plan to name is ready, willing and able to do the job. The Will Book requires you to name one, and only one, guardian (and only one successor guardian) for each child. ▲ Naming a couple as joint guardians raises many problems, including what happens if the couple splits up. If you're nevertheless determined to appoint joint guardians, see a lawyer.

---

[4] In most states a natural parent is entitled to custody unless the court finds the children would be adversely affected.

[5] There is still prejudice against people who live together, especially in the midwest and south, and a judge might award custody to Elinor because Fred was never married to Susan.

The basic wills in Chapter 11 allow you to name but one guardian for all of your children. This will be satisfactory to most people but, as noted above, there may be reasons why you want to name different guardians for different kids. You'll need a Chapter 12 will to do this.

Name One Personal Guardian For All Children

_____

Personal Guardian

_____

Address

_____

Successor Personal Guardian

_____

Address

Name Different Personal Guardians for Different Children

_____

Personal Guardian

_____

Address

Personal Guardian for_____

_____

Personal Guardian

_____

Address

Personal Guardian for_____

_____

Successor Personal Guardian

_____

Address

Successor Personal Guardian for_____

_____

Successor Personal Guardian

_____

Address

Successor Personal Guardian for_____

1. State the Reasons You Named Your Personal Guardian(s)

In the space below, you have the opportunity to state why you named the person(s) you chose as a guardian(s). If you do this, you must assemble your own will using Chapter 12 rather than use a basic will from Chapter 11. The statement which you draft here will be entered in your will draft at that time. As discussed, a statement is wise if your circumstances are unusual and you believe your choice might be challenged, or, if you've appointed different guardians for different children.

Here is an example of such a statement:

"I have nominated my companion, Peter N., to be the guardian of my daughter, Melissa, because I know he would be the best guardian for her. For the past six years Peter has functioned as Melissa's parent, living with me and her, helping to provide and care for her, and loving her. She loves him and regards him as her father. She hardly knows her actual father, Tom D. She has not seen him for four years. He has rarely contributed to her support or taken any interest in her."

_____

_____

_____

_____

_____

_____

C. Property of Your Minor Children

Your minor children cannot own property outright, free of supervision, beyond a minimal amount (often in the $1,000 to $5,000 range depending on the state). This means there must be an adult legally responsible for supervising and administering property owned by a child, including property you leave in your will. You should accordingly use your will to name the adult(s) who are to be responsible for supervising any valuable property owned by your children.

In doing this, there are two basic types of property you should be concerned with. One is property you plan to leave your child in your will. The other is property which your children may acquire in other ways (e.g., inherit from other people, earn, or receive as a personal injury award, etc.). For property you leave to a child in a will, you may want to establish a trust and select a trustee to manage it for the child's benefit until he or she reaches a certain age. For property acquired by your children from other sources, however, a property guardian will be necessary, assuming there is no surviving parent to assume this function. This property guardian, who may in some states also be referred to as the "guardian of the estate," is usually the same person as the one named to care for your children (the "personal guardian"). The property guardian can also be, and often is, the same person as the trustee of your children's trust (assuming you establish one in your will). If all of this sounds a little confusing, that's because it is. However, if you read the rest of Section C carefully before making any decisions, it should become clear.

1. Name a Property Guardian for Your Minors' Property

You should name a property guardian for your minor children, even if you also decide to leave them property in a trust (discussed in Section C(2)). This is because, as noted above, should you die and your minor children receive property from some other source than your will, you want to be sure the money will be managed by someone you've chosen, not a person appointed by a judge later. Also, as I'll discuss below, there are situations where you won't want to establish a trust for property you give to one or more children. If you decide against using a trust, property you give to your minor children will also be managed by the property guardian.

Who do you name for this position? Normally, you name the same person you nominated to be the children's personal guardian. Legally, you can name a different person, but this can lead to coordination problems and may prove confusing to your children. I recommend that you name the same person as personal guardian and property guardian unless the personal guardian is truly inept at managing money.

The property guardian you select normally needs only to be able to administer the child's prop - erty conscientiously and make good sensible decisions about how to take care of the assets wisely. You don't need a financial wizard. A guardian has the power to hire financial professionals to do such jobs as prepare tax returns or give investment advice. Obviously, it's also important that the property guardian be willing to do the job. And you should pick a property guardian who is a resident of your state. Some courts do not recognize an out-of-state property guardian, or require one to post a bond. If you strongly desire to choose an out-of-state property guardian, select someone living in your state as the successor property guardian. Then, if your first choice is prevented from serving, your successor property guardian can serve. Finally, to the extent possible, choose someone the other members of your family respect. Should you die, you want your children to inherit money, not family squabbles.

Example: Martha, a divorced parent with custody of her daughters Alice and Brenda, knows and accepts that her ex-husband Bill will gain custody of her daughters if she dies. Martha's will leaves all her property (worth over a hundred thousand dollars) to her two children. Martha knows Bill is loving, but is a total airhead when it comes to money. So Martha specifies that her sister, Betty, is to be property guardian. This nomination of Betty is normally binding, and Bill cannot have it upset in a court proceeding.[6]

Okay, it's time to record your decisions again. In the space below, put down your choice for property guardian of your minor childrens' estate. Also name a successor property guardian, in case the first guardian named is unable to serve. Remember, these can be and often are the same people who you named as personal guardians (and successor personal guardian). If they are, simply put P.G. (Personal Guardian) to remind you of this fact when you prepare your will in Chapter 11 or 12.

Property Guardian (if same as personal guardian, simply put "P.G.")

Address

Successor Property Guardian

Address

In some unusual circumstances a person wants to name different property guardians for different minor children. You'll need a Chapter 12 will if you want to do this. If you do, complete the following:

Property Guardian

Address

Property Guardian for

---

[6]Bill could try to have Betty's guardianship voided by a court on the grounds it is not in the best interests of the children, but the likelihood any court would do this is very slim.

Property Guardian

Address

Property Guardian for

Successor Property Guardian

Address

Successor Property Guardian for

Successor Property Guardian

Address

Successor Property Guardian for

2. State Reasons You Named Your Property Guardian

In the space below, state the reasons you named your property guardian if there's reason to do this, such as naming different property guardians for different people. If you want to include this in your will, you'll need one from Chapter 12.

3. Leaving Your Minor Children Property in a Trust

Even though you've appointed a property guardian, if your will leaves a substantial amount of property to one or more of your minor children, you would be well advised to put that property in a trust. Also, if you leave substantial property first to your spouse, and then to your minor chil - dren as alternate beneficiaries, you will generally also want to use a trust, which will only become effective in the event your spouse fails to survive you by the period indicated in the will, or you and your spouse suffer a simultaneous death. A trust is an arrangement under which a person called a "trustee" is charged with the responsibility of handling money or property which is actually owned by someone else (i.e., your child), called a "beneficiary." Trusts offer the most desirable way to leave substantial amounts of property to your children because:

• They do not normally require any court supervision, unlike property guardianships (which do on occassion);

• A guardianship must end at age 18 (or whatever age at which your state declares children are no longer minors), whereas legally a trust can last longer, ending when the beneficiary reaches the age set by you in the trust. However, as discussed below, a minor's trust prepared from the Will Book must end no later than when the child reaches age 30;

• Trusts are well-recognized legal forms, and the trustee's authority will usually not be questioned.

Despite this, there are some circumstances where a minor's trust is not advisable. These are:

• If the value of the property being left to a child is small (generally, less than $25,000). In this situation, the annual cost of administering the trust (such as the cost of preparing and filing state and federal income tax returns) will eat up an unacceptably large percentage of the property. If you don't set up a trust, the guardian you name manages the property until the child is 18, at which point your child gets it outright.

• If most or even a substantial part of the property you are leaving a child consists of heir - looms and tangible objects that you want the child to receive free of trust. The children's trust in the Will Book is an all or nothing proposition; if you choose the trust option for a minor child, all property you leave to the child is left through the trust. Therefore, consider carefully whether you really need a trust which runs the risk of tying up the heirlooms but doesn't accomplish much worthwhile since the rest of your property just isn't worth that much.

A trust for minor children is included in the Chapter 11 form wills for persons with minor children, and is set forth in Chapter 12, in Section D, clause r. If you don't want a trust for any of your children, simply cross out all the trust provisions before the final typing of your will.

Under the trust established in a will prepared from the Will Book, the property of each child for whom a trust is selected is held in a separate trust, which ends when the child becomes 30 unless you choose a younger age. Age 30 was selected as a reasonable cut-off age since by then the person should be financially responsible.

▲ There is nothing to legally stop you from choosing an older age than 30 to designate as the age at which the trust ends and the beneficiary gets the property. However, do not select an older age unless you consult with a lawyer. My reason for saying this is that while the sort of simple trust I include here is well-suited to delay the age at which a child takes property for a few years, it may be less well-suited to provide for the lifetime management of money, particularly for an incapacitated or improvident person.

Establishing a separate trust for each child means that the trustee can use some or all of a particular child's property to care for that child, as this may prove necessary. However, one child's property may not be used for the benefit of another. Similarly, the income earned by one child's property held in trust is accumulated for the benefit of that child and may not be distributed to or spent on another child.

▲ There are some situations where you might want a different type of trust than the one presented in the Will Book, and you'll have to consult a lawyer. These situations include:

• You want to create a trust for a child who will be an adult when you die;

• You want to lump all your children's property in a single trust (often called a "family pot trust") so the trustee has the power to divide all property in the trust between your children as she decides is best. A family pot trust lasts until the youngest child reaches the age for termination of the trust. Also, it often involves difficult tax accounting problems and complex personal problems for the trustee (who must choose how to distribute the trust property among the children).

• You want to place extensive controls over the use of property in the trust;

• You want to use a trust for tax planning;

• A child is disabled and requires special care which you want to describe and control.

Now is the time to decide (at least tentatively) whether you want to create a simple trust for any of your minor children, and if so, when you want the trust to end. Enter this information in the chart below. Then, when you draft your will later in the book (Chapter 11 or Chapter 12), you can transfer this information to the appropriate clauses.

Name of child for whom trust is designed	Age trust is to terminate (between18 and 30)

4. Choosing the Trustee

You must name a trustee to manage your children's trust (assuming you decide to create one). If you're married, or living with a mate, and creating a trust to handle simultaneous death, you'll name someone other than your spouse as trustee. The trustee should almost always be the same person as you designated as the children's property guardian, and will commonly be the person you designated as both the personal and property guardian. In other words, in most situations you will be selecting one person who will wear three hats when caring for the person and property of your minor children. You should also name a successor trustee, in case your first choice is unable to serve as trustee during the life of the trust. Again, this can be the same person you designated as successor property guardian.

The duties of a trustee need not be onerous. A trustee may delegate or pay for help to handle the more technical aspects of financial management. Thus, it is routine for a trustee to turn all tax and accounting functions over to a CPA. The trustee's main responsibility is to act honestly and in the best interests of the beneficiaries. If you pick someone with integrity and common sense, the trust will probably be in good hands.

"PETER WOULD BE A BETTER COMPANION BECAUSE HE LOVES THEM AND REGARDS THEM AS HIS OWN."

It is rarely a good idea to pick a bank or other institution as trustee. Most banks won't accept a trust with less than $200,000 of liquid assets and they charge fees for every little act. If you have ever been annoyed that a hospital charged $25 for giving you an aspirin, you will surely be equally upset to read a bank's trust management statement.

As with naming a property guardian, you should pick a trustee who is a resident of your state. Courts in some states do not recognize an out-of-state trustee and instead appoint an in-state trustee. If you strongly desire to choose an out-of-state trustee, select someone living in your state to serve as successor trustee.

Whomever you choose to be trustee, you obviously need to get her consent first. This will also give you a chance to discuss, in general terms, how you would like the trust to be managed.

Example: Ralph and Ariadne agree that Ariadne's sister, Penny, should be personal guardian of their kids should they both die, but that the $400,000 worth of stock the three kids will inherit might better be handled by someone with more business experience. Accordingly, in both of their wills they name Penny as personal guardian of the children, but also create a trust for the property. They name Ralph's sister, Phyllis (who has some investment and business experience), as the trustee, after securing her consent. (Phyllis is also named as property guardian to handle other property belonging to the children.) Ralph's father consents to be the successor trustee and successor property guardian.

Name the Trustee of Your Children's Trust

In the space below, list the person(s) who will be trustee(s) and successor trustees of your children's trust, if for some reason you want different persons than the property guardians.

_____
Trustee (if same as personal/property guardian, simply put "P.G.")

_____
Trustee's Address

_____
Successor Trustee

_____
Successor Trustee's Address

D. Children Not Provided for in a Parent's Will and Disinheritance

Special rules protect children (and children of a deceased child) who are not mentioned or provided for in a parent's will from being accidentally disinherited. The legalese for such children is "pretermitted heirs." It's not that you can't exclude or disinherit a child or grandchild from your will if you wish. You can. It's simply that laws on the books in most states require you to do it explicitly.

Although the specifics vary somewhat from state to state, the general rule can be stated as follows: If your will fails to either mention or provide for one or more of your children, or the children of a child who has died before you (called a "predeceased child"), such children and/or grandchildren are entitled to some of your property by operation of law. In addition, the laws of most states protect your children who are born after the making of the will ("afterborn children") by entitling them to a similar automatic share of your estate.

Overlooked or afterborn children inherit the share of the estate which they would have received had you died intestate—that is, without a will. It may be fine for children (or grandchildren who survive a deceased child) to receive a share of your estate if you really did forget to include them, but it can play havoc with your intentions if you didn't mention them precisely because you did not wish them to inherit anything.

To help you make sure your will and property won't become enmeshed in a pretermitted heir problem, all wills prepared from this book ask you to name all your living children, whether natural, adopted or born out of wedlock (discussed in detail in the next section), and all living children of any child who has previously died. All children and grandchildren thus listed should either be provided for in your will (any amount will do) or specifically disinherited. If you do want to specifically disinherit any of your children (or children of a deceased child), you must do so explicitly. For example, "I disinherit my son, Arthur Jones, and direct that he receive nothing from my estate."

If you wish to do this, you will need to prepare a Chapter 12 will.

Important: If, after preparing your will, you have an additional child (or children), you must revise your will by providing for that new child in it (or disinheriting that child).

If a child dies, leaving children (i.e., your grandchildren), you should then revise your will to provide for (or disinherit) these grandchildren.

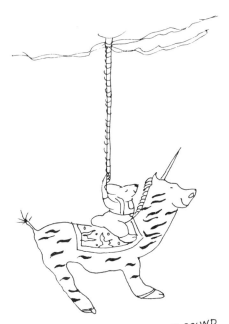

FIRST RIDE ON THE MERRY GO ROUND

E. Adopted and Illegitimate Children

For centuries, courts have been confronted with the issue of whether a gift to "my children" includes adopted children and/or children born out of wedlock. In general, judges attempt to deter - mine what was intended by the person making the will. Unfortunately, this is often not clear. Most states automatically consider persons adopted while they were minors as "children" for the purpose of a gift to "children." This is also true of the situation where a "child" has been adopted after he or she is already an adult. This means that if you have legally adopted a child and leave a gift to "my children" in your will, the adopted child will take his share. However, as noted, to avoid any possible problems in this area, all the wills in this book ask you to name your children and either provide for them or expressly disinherit them. When you do, make sure you include any adopted child and there will be no problem.

The rule in respect to children born out of wedlock, however, cannot be so clearly stated. Basically, states recognize an out-of-wedlock child as a "child" of his mother unless the child was formally released by the mother for adoption. However, an out-of-wedlock child is not a "child" of the father unless the father has legally acknowledged the child as his. Just what constitutes legal acknowledgment differs from state to state.[7] Generally speaking, if a father signs a paternity statement or later marries the mother, the child is acknowledged for purposes of inheritance in all states and enjoys the same legal standing as a child born to parents who are married.[8]

Fortunately, if you are the parent of a child born out of wedlock, the Will Book allows you to make sure such child receives exactly what you desire, no more and no less. Again, when you are asked to name each of your children in your will, simply name them all, whether they were born when you were married to your current spouse, a previous spouse, or no spouse at all. Then, leave them what you wish. If you don't want an out of wedlock child to inherit anything at all, list that child's name and expressly disinherit him or her (using a Chapter 12 will).

F. Gifts to Minors Other Than Your Children

Suppose you wish to leave property to a minor who is not your child. As mentioned, because minors are presumed to be unable to wisely manage their own property, all states provide that such property must be managed by a legally authorized adult until the child reaches majority (in most states, age 18). Most states have passed a law known as the Uniform Gift to Minors Act to regulate the procedure by which most personal property can be transferred to a minor. In addition, a number of states are now passing the Uniform Transfers to Minors Act, an updated version that governs the transfer of all types of property, real and personal. Basically, these acts allow you to make a gift to a minor by naming a custodian for that gift, and appointing that person to act "as custodian under the Uniform Gift/Transfers to Minors Act." The authority of the custodian, which is defined in the Act itself, is quite broad. Normally, you simply appoint the child's legal guardian (usually a parent) as custodian.

In Chapter 12 you will find clauses which refer to these Acts when your will passes property to a minor other than your own child. Your will directs your executor to deliver the property to the named custodian.

Example: John, an elderly widower, wishes to give the bulk of his estate to his favorite niece, 10-year-old Sally. He makes out his will with the aid of the Will Book and names her mother as custodian of the gift under the Uniform Transfers to Minors Act. John dies while Sally is still a minor. John's executor will deliver her inheritance to Sally's mother to administer for her benefit until she is no longer a minor.

Although the use of these Chapter 12 clauses is the best way to pass property to a minor (other than your children), you can still name a minor as beneficiary of property under a Chapter 11 basic will. In that event, the property will normally be transferred to the child's guardian to be managed until the minor becomes an adult.

▲ The other method for leaving property to a minor is to establish a trust (see Section C(2) of this chapter). If you want to leave property to minor children other than your own in trust, see a lawyer.

---

[7]This is discussed in detail in Warner & Ihara, *The Living Together Kit* (Nolo Press).

[8]Acknowledging paternity is made easier under the Uniform Parenting Act, adopted by California and several other states, and includes welcoming a child into the house and treating her as your child.

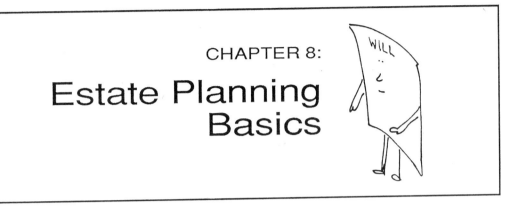

CHAPTER 8:
Estate Planning Basics

One issue you should consider when preparing your will is whether you want to engage in more extensive estate planning. Basically, estate planning is concerned with two problems: avoiding probate and reducing death taxes. It does not offer a more reliable way to transfer prop - erty—just a way to transfer it faster and quite possibly cheaper.

This chapter gives you an overview of the basic estate planning methods so you can decide if you want to investigate the matter further. Experience has taught me that many people want no more than a will, which achieves their primary goal of being sure their property goes to the peo - ple or organizations they want to have it. In other words, they simply don't want to bother learn - ing about the intricacies of estate planning. For example, many younger people rely on a will to dispose of their property should they die unexpectedly and put off worrying about estate planning until they're older. No one can sensibly claim this is a wrong choice. If you're sure now that all you want is a will, you can skip this chapter and get on with preparing it.

In the next several pages I summarize the common techniques used for probate avoidance and estate tax reduction. Please realize, however, that because of space considerations I only provide an overview here. A good source of more sophisticated information (I say modestly) is my book, called *Plan Your Estate: Wills, Probate Avoidance, Trusts & Taxes* (Nolo Press). This book treats these questions thoroughly and I believe that anyone with even a moderate-sized estate will benefit by reading it. Although published in two editions, specifically for California and Texas, the general information it contains on estate planning is of value in all states.

A. Probate

As has been mentioned, property left by a will must go through probate, with the major exceptions noted in Section B(2) of this chapter, which are primarily related to very small estates and those estates left to a surviving spouse. "Probate" is the legal process that includes filing the decedent's will with a court, locating and gathering his assets, paying off his debts and death taxes, and (eventually) distributing what's left as the will directs. If a decedent does not leave a will, or if his will is not valid, the estate will undergo probate through similar "intestacy" proceedings. The major difference between the probate of a will and the probate of an estate under "intestate succes - sion" laws is that in the former instance the property is left as you direct and in the latter it goes to relatives mandated by the law of your state.

1. Drawbacks of Probate

Probate certainly has its drawbacks. The probate process often takes six to nine months, commonly a year, and sometimes even longer. Further, probate normally requires lawyers, which automatically means that the cost goes up. The fees of the attorney and executor are paid from the estate property. Either by law or custom, in many states the fees of the attorney who takes your estate through the probate court are a fixed percentage of the probate estate's value. Moreover, in many states the fees are computed from the estate's total market value.

Let's take an example from California. If Harry dies with a gross estate—that is, the total value of everything he owns, without subtracting debts owed on the property—of $500,000, the attor - ney's fee under the state statute would be $11,150. The fee is based on the $500,000 figure, even if Harry's house has a $100,000 mortgage on it.[1]

2. Reducing Probate Fees

Clearly, where probate fees are based on the size of the probate estate, you can reduce the fees by reducing the probate estate's worth. It is both legal and safe to avoid probate. One approach to reducing probate fees is to transfer the big ticket items of your property—for example, your house, and stock portfolio—outside of probate, and only transfer the less valuable items by your will (see Section C below). Remember, most property transferred by a will (or by intestacy proceedings) is subject to probate while property transferred by probate avoidance devices is not.

Probate fees can also be reduced if the attorney who handles the work agrees to take less than the statutory fee. State statutory fee schedules based on a percentage of the probate estate are not mandatory—no matter what a lawyer may indicate. Attorneys can handle probate on an hourly fee basis, which can result in a much lower fee than the statutory schedule. There's one glitch here. The executor of the will is the person legally responsible for selecting the probate attorney. The will writer cannot, legally, hire the probate attorney because the attorney must be responsible to a living person, not a deceased one. However, since the will writer and the executor are, presumably,

---

[1] This example comes from the California edition of *How To Settle a Simple Estate,* by Julia Nissley (Nolo Press). The author estimates that if Harry's will left everything to his children and one of them acts as executor and probated the estate without an attorney, the process could be accomplished through the mail for approximately $650.

close and trusting, in reality, the will writer can often negotiate a fee agreement with a particular attorney and request the executor to abide by it. The executor will very likely do so.

B. Do You Need To Avoid Probate?

1. How Much Is In Your Probate Estate?

You will probably wish to calculate the value of your property that will pass through probate (called your "probate estate") to determine how much effort it's worth expending to transfer it outside of probate. It's simple to do. Turn to the chart listing your property in Chapter 5, Section B and follow these steps (assuming you used the Chapter 5 Inventory Chart):

Step One: Exclude out all property which will be transferred by means other than your will.

Step Two: Calculate the value of your probate estate by computing the market value for all items of property remaining. In other words, value your house, car, land in the country, boat, etc., as if you owned them free and clear. This number will be larger than the net value of these items, unless you don't owe any money on any of them, in which case it will be the same.

If the result of your calculation indicates that property of substantial value is still included in your estate, consider what additional property, if any, can easily be removed from your probate estate so that your probate fees will be minimized. As mentioned, a living trust is often a good way to accomplish this.

2. Special State Law Exemptions from Probate

Many states have laws which allow a certain amount of property, usually in the $30,000-$60,000 range, to be left by will (or by intestate succession) either free of probate or subject only to a simple, informal, do-it-yourself probate process. The details of these laws vary significantly from state to state.

▲ If you are interested in exploring whether your state exempts small estates from probate, see a lawyer or research the question yourself (see Chapter 9, Section C).

Many states also simplify or eliminate probate for property left by one spouse to the other. So, if you plan to leave all, or most, of your property to your spouse, check to see if probate will be required in your state. If not, you don't need to worry about probate avoidance techniques.

C. Why Wills Are Necessary

Before discussing the principal probate avoidance devices, let's deal with an obvious question: "If a will puts property into the probate system and this results in delays and substantial attorney fees, why have one at all if there are good alternatives?" As mentioned earlier, there are a number of good reasons. Among them are:

• A will is an easy way to make a quick estate plan which can be elaborated on later as you get more property. Probate avoidance techniques pay dividends in the form of saving on probate fees, but obviously they only do this at your death. In the meantime, unfortunately, most of them involve at least some paperwork (e.g., living trusts), and others actually involve your giving up control over some or all of your property (e.g., gifts and joint tenancy). Accordingly, many younger people decide to rely primarily on a will to dispose of their property should they die unexpectedly and wait to make a probate avoiding estate plan until they are older and more settled.

• A will allows you to name a guardian for your children and your children's property, as well as to leave them property in a trust.

• Even if you have provided for your property by some other means than a will, you may end up acquiring valuable property at or shortly before death, such as winning a lottery or receiving back your share of a joint tenancy because of a simultaneous death. So, for this reason alone, a will is extremely valuable to back up other estate planning devices.

• If your estate is modest (in the $30,000-$60,000 range, depending on state law), most states do not require probate or provide simplified and cheap probate procedures. If you are in this cate - gory, there is little need to ever pass property outside of your will.

• In many states, no probate is required to pass property from one spouse to another, so if this is your plan, it is not necessary to plan to avoid probate.

BACK PROBATE BACK!

BEATING BACK PROBATE

D. Probate Avoidance Methods

Here now is a brief review of the principal probate avoidance methods.

1. Living or Inter Vivos Trusts

This is probably the most popular probate avoidance device. Under a living trust ("inter vivos" is Latin for "among the living"), title to property is transferred by its living owner (called a "trustor" or "settlor") to a person or institution (called a "trustee") to hold for a third person (called a "beneficiary"). When the trustor (the person who sets up the trust) dies, the trust property is passed to the named beneficiary under the terms of the trust instrument (the written document establishing the trust) outside of probate.

The attraction of a living trust as a probate avoidance device is that it also allows you (the trustor) to retain full control over your property before you die. Normally the trustor and the trustee are the same person. This allows you, as the owner of property, to put it in a trust com - pletely controlled by you. The trust can be revoked by you at any time for any (or no) reason. Thus, you continue to enjoy the full use of the trust property during your life and can end the trust, sell the property, and spend the money at the races if you choose.

The only real drawback of a living trust as an estate planning device is that certain formalities are required. A formal trust document must be prepared. Title to trust property must be actually transferred to the trust's name. Thus, if you put your house in a living trust, you must properly execute and record a deed transferring ownership to the trust. However, as long as you (the trustor) are also the trustee until you die, no trust income tax returns are required, and separate trust records do not have to be maintained.

Example: James wants to leave his valuable painting collection to his son Bill, but wants total control over it until he dies. He doesn't want the value of his collection, $800,000, included in his probate estate. So he establishes a revocable living trust for the paintings, naming himself as trustee while he lives, and his younger brother to be successor trustee, to act after James' death. James names his son as the trust beneficiary. When James dies, the successor trustee will transfer the paintings to Bill outside of probate. However, should James want to sell a painting, or all the paintings, and end the trust before he dies, he can do so at any time. Similarly, if James subse - quently decides he wants to leave most of the paintings to a museum, he can readily change the trust's beneficiaries to provide for that.

2. Savings Bank Trusts (also called Totten Trusts or a "Pay on Death" Account)

These are a very simple type of living trust. A person (the "trustor") opens a bank account (e.g., checking, savings, certificate, or bank money market) in her name but adds a designation stating that it is in trust for a named beneficiary. Again, the original owner of the money put into the account (the trustor) retains complete and exclusive control over the money until her death, at which point any money left in the account belongs to the named beneficiary without any necessity for probate. If all the money has been withdrawn prior to death, the beneficiary gets nothing. If you want to establish this type of trust, simply visit your bank and complete the appropriate bank forms. They're simple.

3. Joint Tenancy and Tenancy by the Entirety

As discussed in Chapter 4, joint tenancy (or tenancy by the entirety, for a married couple) is a form of shared property ownership where, legally, the surviving owner(s) automatically inherit the interest of a deceased owner through a "right of survivorship." All joint tenancy property is trans - ferred outside of probate when the first joint tenant(s) die. In many states, marital joint tenancy is called tenancy by the entirety.

Joint tenancy is an excellent probate avoidance technique when you are relatively certain about who you want your property to go to and don't anticipate a change of heart. However, it is not as flexible a device as the revocable trust discussed above, since by placing your property in a joint tenancy, you immediately give the other joint tenant(s) equal ownership. That person (or persons) can sell his interest in the property, or it can be attached by creditors. Also, placing your property in joint tenancy with someone else is a legal gift (unless you sell her the share), and may require the filing of a gift tax return if you give away property worth more than $10,000 to a particular person in a calendar year.

Okay, now that you know what joint tenancy is, the question is do you already own property in joint tenancy? If you are concerned with real estate, look at the deed. If it says: "To John and Sarah Jones, in joint tenancy," or "As tenants by the entirety," it's clear. If the deed says, "To John and Arthur Jones as tenants in common," then it's just as clear that you are not joint tenants. Tenancy in common, another traditional form of co-ownership, does not carry with it rights of survivorship.[2]

What if your deed says, "To John and Arthur Jones"? Is this a joint tenancy or tenancy in common? The answer is that most states presume it is a tenancy in common, reasoning that if the co-owners wanted to create a right of survivorship, they would have explicitly said so in the deed. Similarly, if the persons whose names are listed on the deed are married, community property states will generally treat the property as community property, which means you and your spouse are each free to dispose of one-half of it.[3]

Can personal property (all property that isn't real estate) be held in joint tenancy? Generally yes, so long as there is a written document to that effect. Joint tenancy bank accounts, for exam - ple, require a written form which is signed by the joint tenants and which specifies the account as a joint tenancy. If you don't know whether your shared account fits this description, ask your bank. Likewise, automobiles, securities and business interests can be held in joint tenancy by appropriate registration on the ownership documents with the Motor Vehicles Department.

4. Gifts

As you know by now, the phrase "gifts" as used so far in this book means property left by a will. However, as you also know, the word "gifts" has another meaning, which is any property transferred freely, without commercial intent, from one living person to another (or to an organ - ization). It's this meaning of the word "gifts" that is discussed here.

---

[2]A tenant in common can, and should, use a will or other estate planning device, such as a living trust, to dispose of her share of such property, since it won't pass automatically to the other owner(s) upon her death.

[3]California and several other states make it very easy for one spouse to transfer community property to the other by will with only very minimal after-death formalities.

Property given away at any time before death is not part of the probate estate upon death. For property to be considered a gift, the person giving it needs to actually surrender ownership and control of the property while he is living.

5. Life Insurance

Assuming that you designate a specific beneficiary in your life insurance policy, the proceeds of the policy pass under the terms of the policy rather than under the terms of your will and therefore do not go through probate. Accordingly, the purchase of life insurance policies is a popular way to avoid probate. However, if for some reason a person designates her estate (as opposed to a person or institution), as the beneficiary of the policy, which is rarely done, the proceeds would be part of the probate estate.

Note on Planning and Probate Avoidance: Transferring some, or all, of your property outside of probate can raise questions and problems you need to anticipate. If you have debts, how are they to be paid? Similarly, how are death taxes to be paid? Since this isn't a book on estate planning, I don't discuss those matters in detail here.[4]

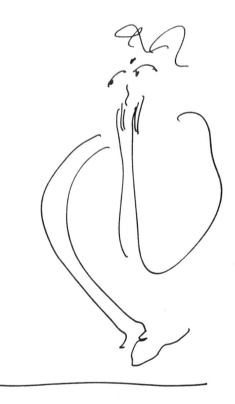

PROBATE

---

[4]However, I do cover these concerns in detail in my book, *Plan Your Estate* (Nolo Press) for Californians and Texans.

E. Estate Planning to Reduce Taxes

At death, all property owned by you is subject to a federal estate tax (and state death taxes, if your state has them) unless it is exempt under the statutes. This is true not only for property passed by your will, but also for property passed at death outside of probate, such as property placed in joint tenancy or in a living trust or bank account trust. Only if you have actually surren - dered control over your property, as well as title to it, prior to death will the taxing authorities consider it outside your estate. However, gifts made during your lifetime are subject to gift taxes, which are basically the same as estate taxes, except you may give away $10,000 per person per year free of any tax.

One primary goal of sophisticated estate planning is to either reduce the amount of death taxes by giving property away before you die or leaving property in a way that results in the minimum possible taxation. For those with small, or moderate, estates, roughly anyone with property worth less than $1,000,000, there are only a few possible means to reduce taxes, which are discussed here. If your estate is in the $1,000,000 class or above, you will be wise to invest a few of those dollars in a consultation with a tax attorney, accountant, or both.

1. Many Estates Are Exempt from Taxation

Before worrying about reducing death taxes, be sure you need to bother with the matter at all.

In 1987 and thereafter, federal estate law exempts from tax estates of less than $600,000.[5] Further, all property left to a surviving spouse is exempt. So, in general, if your anticipated net estate is less than $600,000, and you have not given away large amounts of property (above $10,000 per person per year) while living, you do not need to worry about how to reduce federal taxes and should proceed directly to Section F. If, on the other hand, either your estate alone, or the combined value of your own and your spouse's estate, if you are leaving most of your property to her, is expected to be larger than these amounts, then thought as to how to reduce your taxes is warranted. This is because the federal estate tax rates are stiff. They start at 37% for non-exempt property.

What about state death taxes? A number of states, including the most populous, California, don't have any. Many that do exempt substantial amounts of property.[6] Perhaps most impor - tantly, state death tax rates are much lower than the federal rates. So even if your state is subject to state death taxes, the bite taken is relatively small. In general, this means it's not worth the bother and cost to try to reduce only state death taxes. If you want to double-check this, find out from your state's taxing authorities what rules affect you.

Let's now turn to some of the methods commonly used to reduce federal estate taxes.

---

[5] ▲ Certain types of property do not have to be valued at their "best use" market value for federal estate tax purposes. These include family farmland and wooded land. Also, an estate can have up to 14 years to pay off estate taxes on a closely held business if the value of your interest in it exceeds 35% of the value of your estate. If you have any of these kinds of property, consult a lawyer before finalizing your will.

[6] Thus New York and many other states exempt all property transferred to a surviving spouse.

2. Gifts

One way to reduce the size of your estate and save on estate taxes is to transfer your property while you are still alive. As mentioned, you may give $10,000 to any person free of gift taxes each year. Your spouse may do the same. Thus, if a couple has three children, they could each give $10,000 to each child each year, thus transferring $20,000 free of federal gift tax per child and removing this amount from their estate. In ten years, a total of $600,000 could be transferred in this way tax-free. Indeed, this would probably result in your saving a much larger sum because of the interest and dividends this money would earn which would, absent a gift, have ended up in your estate. With a gift, the interest and dividends will instead be earned by the people to whom you give the money and whom, presumably, are in a lower income tax bracket.[*]

Another kind of property suitable for gifts is ownership of a life insurance policy. The value of the proceeds from life insurance is included in the taxable estate of the decedent (i.e., the person insured) if he was the legal owner of the policy at his death. If the policy has a large pay-ment—say in the hundreds of thousands of dollars range—inclusion of that sum in the taxable estate can result in federal estate taxes, or additional taxes. The taxes attributable to the insurance proceeds can be eliminated by the insured's gift of the policy to someone else. Under IRS regulations, this must be done at least three years prior to the insured's death. Note that the beneficiary is not the owner of the policy. The owner is the person who pays for the policy, has the right to name the beneficiary, etc.

3. Irrevocable Trusts

There are a number of ways that irrevocable trusts can be used to save on death taxes. An irrevocable trust is one that cannot be revoked or altered (except in very narrow circumstances defined by the terms of the trust). A living trust, in contrast, can be revoked as long as the person who set it up is alive. Only when he dies does that trust becomes irrevocable and the property pass to the beneficiary. Here are some examples of uses of irrevocable trusts for tax savings:

(a) Each member of a married couple sets up a trust for his or her property with their children (or other loved ones) as the ultimate beneficiaries, with the surviving spouse receiving the trust income during his or her life. This is called a "life estate" trust. This is an alternative to each spouse leaving money to the other outright and paying a hefty estate tax on the amount of the combined property over $600,000 when the second spouse dies.

(b) A person establishes a trust for the benefit of grandchildren (with the income to go to your children during their lives) instead of leaving the money directly to the children and having them pass the money along when they die. This is called a "generation-skipping trust." Under a special Internal Revenue Code provision, your estate pays an estate tax when you die, but no additional tax is owed when the children die and the grandchildren get the money. A total of $1,000,000 can be passed in this way. Obviously, establishing this sort of trust only makes sense if your children have enough money so they can get along with only the interest, not the principal of this million dollars.

▲ Irrevocable trusts should be drafted by an attorney. The IRS regulations applicable to irrevocable trusts are complicated. A mistake can cost you all the tax savings you'd planned for. Also, irrevocable trusts are designed to last for quite a while, which means there must be full consideration of contingencies over time.

---

[*]Under the 1986 Tax Reform Act, income from gifts by adults to children under 14 is taxed at the adult's tax rate.

4. The Marital Exemption and the "Second Tax"

All property transferred from one spouse to another at death is exempt from federal (and usually state) estate tax. This is true even if you leave far more than the $600,000 amount which is exempt from tax from 1987 on. Even so, as noted, it may not be wise to transfer a large estate to an elderly surviving spouse. Why? Because if the survivor has property of his own, and that prop - erty, combined with what you leave, is worth more than $600,000 in 1987, a large and unneces - sary estate tax will have to be paid when the second spouse dies. This is why estate planners refer to this as the "second tax" problem. The larger the estate, the steeper the tax rate.

The point of this discussion is simple—there will be far less total tax liability if the first spouse left all the property, or a portion of it, directly to the children, or established a trust under which the surviving spouse gets the income, but the principal goes to the children or other beneficiary.

Example: Suppose Calvin and Phyllis, husband and wife, each have an estate worth $550,000, i.e., their total combined worth is $1,100,000. Calvin dies in 1988, leaving all his property to Phyllis. Because of the marital exemption, no estate tax is assessed. Phyllis dies in 1989. Her estate is the entire $1,100,000, which she leaves to the children. In 1989, since $600,000 can be left to anyone free of estate tax, $500,000 of the money left to the children is subject to tax. The tax assessed is $155,800.

Now suppose Calvin had not left his property outright to Phyllis, but had established a trust, with Phyllis having a "life estate" in the trust property and Calvin's children being the trust's ultimate beneficiaries. What this means, legally, is that Phyllis has the right to the income and use of the trust property.[7] As trustee, Phyllis can manage the trust property. Except as noted, Phyllis cannot spend the trust principal. She is never the legal owner of the trust property. The trust property is subject to estate tax when Calvin dies, but is not included in Phyllis' taxable estate.

---

[7]Phyllis can be given additional rights, such as the right to receive 5% of the principal annually and the right to use any amount of the principal necessary for her health, welfare, or support.

In this situation there would be no tax liability at all. When Calvin dies (in 1988) he can transfer his $550,000 to anyone, including the trust, free of estate tax. Likewise, when Phyllis dies in 1989, she can transfer her $550,000 to the children free of estate tax.

▲ Preparation of a marital "life estate" trust definitely requires an expert. There are many complexities and options involved (e.g., use of a "Q-Tip" trust, etc.). It simply isn't safe to prepare this trust yourself, unaided.

5. Charities

All property left to legitimate, tax-exempt charities is exempt from federal estate tax. Tech - nically, the amount given to charity is deducted from the net estate, before determining its size for federal estate tax purposes.

F. Estate Planning Designed To Place Controls On Property

For any number of reasons, a person may want to impose controls over property given to beneficiaries. The usual solution is to create a trust imposing the desired controls. I discussed one version of this type of trust in Chapter 7 when I indicated that using this book you can elect to leave money in trust for your children to receive at any age up to 30.

Here are some examples of other uses of trusts for control.

Example 1: Bill wants to leave a significant amount of money to his son, Tim, but worries that Tim is improvident and easily influenced. So Bill leaves the money in a "spendthrift" trust which ends when Tim becomes 50. Until then, the trustee controls distribution of the trust funds to Tim, who cannot legally pledge them or use them before actual receipt.

Example 2: Vivian leaves money for her six grandchildren. She wants the money used where it is most needed, which she realizes she can't determine in advance. So she leaves the money in a "sprinkling" trust, with the trustee having the power to distribute trust monies as she determines the beneficiaries need.

▲ There are many other types of control trusts, such as ones for disadvantaged people, invalids, social causes, etc. All require preparation by a lawyer.

G. Planning for Incapacity: The Durable Power of Attorney

Although not strictly speaking estate planning, it is also sensible to prepare for the contin - gency that you become incapacitated and can no longer handle your own financial affairs or make medical decisions.

The wisest way to plan for incapacity is to prepare what's called a "Durable" Power of Attorney (valid in all states except Illinois, Louisiana and Washington, DC). A durable power of attorney is a document in which you appoint someone else (called your "attorney in fact") to manage your financial and business affairs should you become incapacitated. Normally, a durable power of attorney does not take effect unless and until you do become incapacitated. So it functions as a kind of legal insurance, making sure you are protected, without court proceedings, if you ever need it.

In your durable power of attorney you can make provision for your medical treatment if you are incapacitated and hospitalized. Of paramount concern to many people is the issue of life support systems. If they ever encounter a terminal condition or fatal illness, many people want to die a natural death, rather than having their life artificially prolonged by life support equipment. You can make your desires regarding life support equipment binding by use of a durable power of attorney.

All the information and forms you need to prepare a valid durable power of attorney are in *The Power of Attorney Book* (Nolo Press).

H. Estate Planning—Summing Up

For people with relatively modest amounts of property (say less than $60,000), a will adequately solves all their estate planning problems because their estate will probably neither be subjected to federal estate tax nor probate fees. For larger estates, consideration should be given to the pros and cons of probate avoidance. Are the savings to your inheritors worth the time, effort, and costs involved in probate avoidance? Is a will sufficient for your needs now, with probate avoidance to be considered (much) later?

People with very large estates will find that estate planning involves both making a will and reducing the amount of taxable property passed by it. The more an estate is worth, the more important estate planning becomes. As noted above, even though you will probably want to limit the property you pass by your will, you still need one.

Finally, it's sensible to prepare a durable power of attorney to prepare in advance for what happens if you ever become incapacitated.

CHAPTER 9:

Lawyers and Doing Your Own Legal Resarch

As already discussed, I believe most people can safely prepare their own will by using Nolo's Will Book without any help from a lawyer. However, the decision of whether you want, or need, legal assistance is one only you can make. For a variety of reasons, you may need more information than is presented in this book. Or you may want review of your work by a lawyer to reassure yourself that your will is proper and legal.

A. Do You Need a Lawyer?

Here is a summary of the main reasons the services of a lawyer are usually warranted:

• You want to learn more about a specific area of your state's laws;

• Your estate is in the $1,000,000 range or more and will be subject to a substantial federal estate tax unless you engage in tax planning;

• You want to establish a trust, other than a simple trust for your children;

• You want to give a gift with complex shared ownership, such as a "life estate";

• You own a part of a small business and have questions as to the rights of surviving owners, your ownership share, etc.;

• You must make arrangements for long-term care of a beneficiary (for example, a handicapped child);

• You fear someone will contest your will (on grounds of fraud, undue influence or incompetence);

• You wish to disinherit, or substantially disinherit, your spouse.

B. Working With a Lawyer

For intelligent consumers, consulting with a lawyer should most definitely not mean that you hire one and say, "I want a will, so please prepare one for me." At a minimum, you should take the time to understand your needs, and prepare a rough draft of your own will. Indeed, most readers of this book who do hire a lawyer will probably want their attorney to do little more than resolve specific questions and insure that the finished product achieves their goals. If you decide you want a lawyer to review your draft will, be clear with yourself and the lawyer, on what you expect the lawyer to do. You obviously don't want to let any lawyer cast you in the role of a passive "client" (interestingly, the Latin root of the word client translates as "to obey," or "to hear"). If he tries to do this, it's wise to hire someone else.

1. Paying Your Lawyer

As you already know, lawyers are expensive. They charge by the hour at fees ranging from $75 to $250 per hour. While fancy office trappings, three-piece suits and solemn faces are no guarantee (or even any indication) that a lawyer is one you'll like, this conventional style will almost always insure that you will be charged a fee towards the upper end of this range. Interestingly, at Nolo our experience tells us that high fees and quality service don't necessarily go hand in hand. Indeed, the attorneys I think most highly of tend to charge moderate fees (for lawyers, that is).

Be sure you've settled your fee arrangement at the start of your relationship. Generally, I feel that fees in the range of $75-$100 per hour are fair (given a lawyer's overhead) depending on the area of the country and what you want the lawyer to do. In addition to the amount charged per hour, you also want a clear commitment from the lawyer concerning how many hours he expects to put in on your problem. Often, one office consultation is all you need. If a lawyer tells you wills are complex and it will take him many hours to handle your problems, go somewhere else.

2. Finding a Lawyer

All this sounds good, you may think, but how do you find a lawyer? Believe me, this isn't difficult. Indeed, ours is such a lawyer-ridden society that it's something of a miracle if one hasn't already found you. The trick, of course, is not just finding (or being found by) any lawyer, but retaining one who is trustworthy, competent, and charges fairly. A few words of advice may be helpful.

First, decide what type of lawyer you need. This depends on what your problem is. If you want to engage in sophisticated estate planning, especially the creation of trusts to save on estate taxes (discussed in Chapter 8), see someone who specializes in the field. She may charge relatively high fees, but if she's good, she's worth it. And if you need this sort of estate planning help, you pre - sumably have somewhere around $1,000,000 or more and can afford it. Irrevocable trusts are quite technical. Most general practice lawyers are simply not sufficiently educated in this field to hire them to do this type of work. On the other hand, for other needs, such as a general review of a will, or a check of some provision of your state's laws, a competent attorney in general practice is more than adequate.

Next, it's important that you feel a personal rapport with your lawyer. You want one who treats you as an equal. When talking with a lawyer on the phone, or at the first conference, ask some specific questions. If the lawyer answers them clearly and concisely—explaining, but not talking down to you—fine. If he acts wise, but says little except to ask that the problem be placed in his hands (with the appropriate fee, of course), watch out. You are either talking with someone who doesn't know the answer and won't admit it (common), or someone who finds it impossible to let go of the "me expert, you peasant" way of looking at the world (even more common).

To find a lawyer you'll like (and who'll do a good job), the best route is the traditional one—ask your friends. If you've got a close friend who found a lawyer he liked, chances are you'll like her too. Otherwise you've got a problem. Here are some suggestions on how you can find a lawyer you'll be pleased with:

• Check with people you know who own their own businesses. Almost anyone running a small business has a relationship with a lawyer. Chances are they've found one they like. If this lawyer doesn't handle wills, he'll know someone who does. And, best of all, because he has a continuing relationship with your friend, he has an incentive to recommend someone who is good, not just his brother-in-law who owes him money.

• Check with people you know in any political or social organization you're involved with. They may well know of a competent lawyer whose attitudes are similar to yours.

• Be cautious when dealing with bar association referral panels. Never assume a bar association referral is a seal of approval. While lawyers are supposed to be screened as to their specialty to get on these panels, screening is usually perfunctory. Often the main qualification is that the lawyer needs business.

Question the lawyer and make your own judgment, just as you would if you got the referral any other way.

• Check the classified ads under "Attorneys." Young attorneys just starting out often advertise low rates to build up a practice. Also, there are quite a few attorneys around who are no longer interested in handling court-contested matters but do provide consultations at low rates. This could be just what you need.

• Don't be afraid to shop around. Talk to a lawyer personally so you can get an idea of how friendly and sympathetic she is to your concerns. Explain that you've drafted your own will and what you want the attorney to do.

C. Doing Your Own Research

There's a viable alternative to hiring a lawyer to resolve legal questions that affect your will—you can do your own legal research. This can provide some real benefits for those willing to learn how to do it. Not only will you save some money, you'll gain a sense of mastery over an area of law, generating a confidence that will stand you in good stead should you have other legal prob-lems. For example, as discussed in Chapter 8, you may want to know whether small estates are exempt from probate in your state and, if so, at what level.

Fortunately, researching wills and related issues is an area generally well suited to doing your own legal research. Most questions do not involve massive or abstruse legal questions. Often you need only check the statutes of your state to find one particular provision. Or you can learn how to use legal form books, the very books lawyers often refer to in order to solve a problem.

If you decide you want to do your own research, how do you go about it? First, it surely helps to have a research aid. If you can't hire your own law librarian, the best book explaining how to do your own legal work is Elias, *Legal Research: How To Find and Understand the Law* (Nolo Press). It tells you all you need to know to do effective research.

Next, locate a law library (or a public library with a good law collection). There's usually one in your principal county courthouse. These law libraries are normally supported by your tax dol-lars or by the fees paid to file legal papers, and are open to the public. The librarians in county law libraries are generally most helpful and courteous to nonlawyers who wish to learn to do their own legal research. Ask them how you can locate the state's statutes (these are called "codes," "laws," "statutes," depending on the state). Usually what you want is called the "annotated ver-sion," which contains both your state's statutes and excerpts from any relevant judicial decisions and cross references to related articles and commentaries.

Once you have found your state's statutes, check the index for provisions dealing with wills or a specific subject that concerns you. Generally, you will find what you want in the volume of statutes dealing with your state's basic civil or probate laws. These are usually called a name such as "Civil Code" or "Probate Laws." These codes are numbered sequentially, and once you get the correct number in the index, it's easy to find the statute you need. If you have trouble, the law librarian will usually be happy to help.

Once you have looked at the basic statutes contained in the hardcover volume, and checked the pocket part at the back of the book for any amendments, you will probably want to skim the summaries of recent court decisions contained in the "Annotation" section immediately following the statute itself. If a summary looks like it might help answer your question, you will want to read the full court opinion which the summary was taken from.

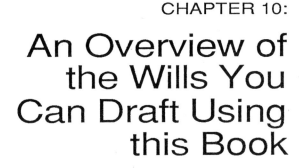

CHAPTER 10:

An Overview of the Wills You Can Draft Using this Book

A. How to Proceed

Now that you've assembled all the personal information you need to prepare your will, it's time to focus on actually preparing it. Unfortunately, no one generic will form suits all needs. Recognizing this, the Will Book offers two basic formats for you to draft your will:

1. Six basic fill-in-the-blank will forms for use in many common situations. These are set out and explained in Chapter 11; and

2. A set of will clauses which you select to be included in your will. This assemble-it-yourself will format, set out in Chapter 12, allows somewhat more flexibility in choosing what to include in your will.

To help you decide which format is best for you, let's briefly examine these two approaches to will drafting.

B. Basic Form Wills

If your desires are straightforward, one of the six basic wills set out in Chapter 11 will probably meet your needs. These are specifically designed for the following personal situations:

I. Will for a single person with no minor children[1]

II. Will for a single person with minor children

III. Will for a husband or wife with no minor children[2]

IV. Will for a husband or wife with minor children

V. Will for a person who lives with a lover/mate and who has no minor children[3]

VI. Will for a person who lives with a lover/mate and who has minor children

You can use a Chapter 11 will to achieve such fundamental purposes of will writing as:

• Making gifts of all your personal and real property to named beneficiaries;

• Naming an alternate beneficiary for each gift in case the first beneficiary you name fails to survive you by 45 days;

• Naming a residuary beneficiary (and an alternate residuary beneficiary) to receive any property not specifically given to named beneficiaries;

• Appointing persons to care for the persons and property of your minor children;

• Establishing a 45-day survivorship period for beneficiaries;

• Setting up a trust for your children, and

• Appointing your executor.

As I indicate in Chapter 11, you can alter the printed text of a fill-in-the-blanks will to make minor technical changes, but the text of the will shouldn't be revised or changed in major ways. If after you review the wills in Chapter 11 you find that one or more of your basic desires cannot be accommodated, check to see whether Chapter 12 will meet your needs.

C. Assemble-It-Yourself Wills

In Chapter 12 you have the opportunity to assemble your will clause by clause. Where there are sensible alternatives to handling a particular legal need, I provide you with a choice of different clauses, with accompanying explanations. This approach allows you to address all the concerns covered in Chapter 11 wills, plus the following matters which are not covered in a Chapter 11 basic will:

• Specifying how your probate costs and death taxes are to be paid. This subject is not covered explicitly in the Chapter 11 wills. In many states, this means that all probate costs and death taxes are pro-rated between beneficiaries according to the percentage of the total worth of your property they receive. But if you want to be more definite about this, use a clause from Chapter 12;

• Appointing co-executors;

---

[1]This form is also approprite for a single person with no children or with adult children only.

[2]This form is also appropriate for a married person with no children or with adult children only.

[3]This form is also appropriate for a person who lives with a mate/lover and who has no children, or who has adult children only.

• Imposing a survivorship period of your choosing on all your beneficiaries. Chapter 11 wills contain a standard 45-day clause. In Chapter 12, you have the opportunity to lengthen or shorten this period;

• Stating why it's in your children's best interest for the person you named as their guardian (of their person and/or property) to be legally appointed;

• Giving particular items of property (especially real estate) free of liens or encumbrances, such as mortgages;

• Forgiving debts;

• Expressly disinheriting a child or child of a deceased child (i.e., your grandhild);

• Making a gift to a minor child other than your own children and specifying an adult custodian of the gift to manage it until the minor becomes an adult;

• Including a no-contest clause in your will. This states that if a person to whom you leave property contests your will, he is disinherited;

• Including provisions in your will regarding body part donations, your funeral, and your burial; and

• Providing for your pets.

THE CHOOSE YOUR WILL FASHION SHOW

Chapter 12 does not attempt to present every conceivable will clause relevant to every possible issue. To do so would result in a book of encyclopedic length. Chances are, though, that your intentions and goals can be met using the clauses in Chapter 12. If you're the exception to this rule and you need to modify or add to the material presented, you'll have to do your own research or see a lawyer.

D. Formalities

Once you've drafted your will in Chapter 11 or Chapter 12, you will need to accurately and neatly type (or have typed) a final copy. This final copy must then be signed by you in front of three witnesses, who must then in turn sign the will. In Chapter 13 I tell you in detail how to go about each of these tasks.

Once your will is made following the instructions in this book and is properly signed and witnessed, it is valid. This means it will be implemented after your death In some instances, especially those involving small estates, this can often be done by the person you name as executor (personal representative) with no need for formal probate. More typically, your will will be presented to a probate court which will supervise its implementation. To get your will admitted to probate, your executor will have to convince the judge that the will is genuine (i.e., that it's really your will). This is generally accomplished by having one or two of your witnesses testify to that effect, either in person or through a written sworn statement.

In most states, the need for this type of proof can usually be avoided if you and your witnesses appear before a notary public and all sign an affidavit to the effect that your will was properly signed and witnessed. This procedure is aptly called "self proving" your will. If you want to take this additional step, Chapter 13 also provides the proper form and detailed accompanying instructions.

To summarize, your job will be easiest if you can fit your desires within one of the basic wills in Chapter 11. If not, Chapter 12 should do the trick. Whether you use Chapter 11 or Chapter 12, however, you will need to have your will typed, signed and witnessed as I instruct in Chapter 13. If you wish you may choose to make your will "self proving," also as discussed in Chapter 13.

CHAPTER 11:
Basic Wills

A. Introduction

This chapter explains how to complete all the basic fill-in-the-blanks wills. These no-frills, no-fuss wills allow you to:

1. Leave your property to who you want to give it to; this includes your spouse, children, friends, charitable institutions, or anyone else;

2. Name alternate beneficiaries for gifts you make, in case any beneficiary fails to survive you by 45 days;

3. Name a guardian and successor guardian for your minor children;

4. Leave property to one or more of your minor children in a simple trust, so that they get the property at any age between 18 and 30 designated by you;

5. Appoint your executor; and

6. If you're married or part of a couple, provide for the contingency of simultaneous death.

Note on Traditional but Unnecessary Will Language: Because these basic wills are designed for efficient, practical use, they employ a minimum of legalese. This means some traditional but legally unnecessary phrases have been omitted.

B. To Complete Your Basic Will

To complete one of the wills in this chapter, follow these steps:

Step 1. Read sections C, D and E of this chapter to gain an understanding of how the basic will format works.

Step 2. Select the will form from Section F that best fits your needs. There are six to choose from, as follows:

I. Will for a single person with no minor children. (This form is also appropriate for a single person with no children, or with adult children only.)

II. Will for a single person with minor children.

III. Will for a husband or wife with no minor children. (This form is also appropriate for a married person with no children, or with adult children only.)

IV. Will for a husband or wife with minor children.

V. Will for a person who lives with a lover/mate and who has no minor children. (This form is also appropriate for a person living with a mate/lover and who has no children or has adult children only.)

VI. Will for a person who lives with a lover/mate and who has minor children.

These forms are perforated so you can remove the one which fits your situation and conven - iently use it as a worksheet to prepare your draft will.

Note: If you are living with a mate or lover, but are still legally married to somebody else, remember that in most common law states your spouse is entitled to inherit a part of your estate. See Chapter 4. Once you understand your spouse's inheritance rights, you can go ahead and use Will V or Will VI, as appropriate. You may want to see a lawyer before you proceed.

Step 3. Complete the blanks in the will form you've chosen. Here's how to proceed:

• Use a pencil, since you may need to erase mistakes, or make changes (remember, this is your first draft).

• If you need more space than the form provides to complete a particular blank, here's what to do:

  a. Put "continued on Attachment 1" at the end of the too short space on the form.

  b. Title a piece of blank typing paper by marking it "Attachment 1, continuation of Clause ____ ," filling in the number of the clause that's being continued (e.g., "Attachment 1, continuation of Clause 3").

  c. Complete the Attachment by providing all information needed.

  d. Attach the continuation page or pages to your draft.

  e. If you need another attachment for another clause, repeat the process, numbering this Attachment 2.

Step 4. Insert the standard language for the powers of your executor at the place indicated in the basic will. You will find this language set out in a box beginning on page 11:55. I do not repeat all of this standard language in every will because it's both lengthy and exactly the same for each.

Step 5. If you have established a trust for a child or children, insert the standard provisions for the powers of your trustee at the place indicated in your will. You will find these powers set out in a box starting on page 11:56. Again, I do not repeat all this language in all the wills designed for people with children because as with the executor's powers, it's both lengthy and exactly the same for each.

Step 6. If a portion of a will form does not apply to you, simply draw a line through it so your typist will know to leave it out of the final draft. For example, if you have minor children but have decided to leave them property only in care of a guardian and not in a trust (see Chapter 7, Section C), delete the trust provision by drawing a line through it. If you eliminate an entire clause, be sure you renumber the rest of the clauses.

Step 7. When you've filled in the blanks on the will form of your choice, review your draft until you're confident your will does what you want it to. Also use this opportunity to make sure that all personal pronouns (his, hers, theirs, etc.) and references to the singular and plural are correct.

Step 8. Type your will. If you type your will yourself, you should have little trouble under-standing exactly what to include. However, if someone else will type your will, be sure your typist:

• Receives a neatly prepared draft so he or she will not make a mistake as a result of being confused.

• Understands exactly where any attachments are to be inserted in the will;

• Knows to insert the standard language for executor powers at the appropriate place and, if you establish a trust for one or more of your children, also knows where to insert the minor's trust provisions.

• Knows that the instructional words printed on the form below the blank lines and any clauses you've drawn lines through are not to be typed in the final will.

• Understands the rules for format and neatness which are discussed in Chapter 13. Generally, I recommend that your will be typed double-spaced, although this is not a legal requirement. After the will has been typed, carefully proofread it.

Step 9. Depending on the degree of your uncertainty and/or confusion about any of these matters, and the amount of property you have, you may want to have your will checked by an attorney. Do remember, though, that if you can use one of the forms in this chapter and follow all the instructions in this book, your will is probably already in good shape and fully legal.

Step 10. Comply with the signing and witnessing requirements outlined in Chapter 13.

C. What Is Included In a Basic Will Form

Now let's examine the six basic wills included in this chapter by studying each component separately. Remember, as you look at each clause, the places where you are to insert information have blank lines. Do not enter information now. These are only for the purpose of introducing you to our will forms. The actual drafting of your will starts in Section G.

Will Identification Provision

As already stated, your will should identify you by the name you customarily use when you sign legal documents and other important papers. If, for any reason, you've used different names—e.g., you changed your name to Jerry Adams, but still own some property in the name of Jerry Adananossos, identify yourself with both names, as "Jerry Adams A/K/A Jerry Adananossos," and sign your will that way. Providing your address can help eliminate any doubt about the state in which you reside. It also helps establish which county the will is to be probated in.[1]

WILL OF _____ *Denis Clifford* _____.
                          your name

I, _____ *Denis Clifford* _____, a resident of
                  your name

_____ *Berkeley* _____, *Alameda County* _____,
           city   county

_____ *California* _____ declare that this is my will.
              state

Clause 1. Revoke All Previous Wills

This is a standard and necessary clause which revokes all previous wills, including any hand - written ones. To be safe, it is used whether or not you have in fact made another will. A revoca - tion clause helps prevent any possible confusion or litigation regarding the validity of prior wills. All wills in this chapter contain a revocation clause; you don't have to add anything.

1. I revoke all wills and codicils I have previously made.

Clause 2. Name Your Spouse and Children (if any)

If currently married, you should select either Will III (will for a husband or wife with no minor children) or Will IV (will for a husband or wife with minor children). Either way, insert your spouse's name. The clause where you do this states that whenever you refer to your "husband or wife" elsewhere in the will, you are referring to the person named in this clause.

Whether or not you are currently married, each of the six wills in this chapter provides space for you to list the names of former spouses and how the marriage ended (i.e., death, annulment, or divorce).

---

[1]See Chapter 14 for a discussion of when you need to revise your will if you move.

If you use one of the six wills in this chapter, your will must both name and provide for (give something to) all of your children and all children of a deceased child. This includes children of previous marriages, children born out of wedlock, and legally adopted children. If you wish to completely disinherit a child, you must use Chapter 12 to make your will. Otherwise, your estate may face the "pretermitted heir" problem discussed in Chapter 7, Section D.

2. I am married to _____*Patti Jones*_____, and all references in this will to my __*wife*__ are to __*her*__. [If appropriate] I was previously married to _____*Carol Riordan*_____. That marriage was terminated by __*divorce*__. [Repeat if you were married more than once.]

I am the father of the following __*one child*__, whose __*name*__ and __*date*__ of birth is/are:

_____*Michael Jones*_____   _____*2/19/81*_____
Name   Date of Birth

There are ____ living children of my deceased child _____:

_____   _____
Name of Grandchild   Date of Birth

_____   _____
Name of Grandchild   Date of Birth

_____   _____
Name of Grandchild   Date of Birth

Add more lines to the simple will form as needed to list additional former spouses, children and children of deceased children. If there are no living children of a deceased child, draw a line through that provision so it's not included in your final will.

Living Together Note: If you are living with a lover or mate and select Will V (will for a person who lives with a lover/mate and who has no minor children) or Will VI (will for a person who lives with a lover/mate and who has minor children), the clauses in these wills dealing with your significant other use the correct language to recognize your unmarried status.

Clauses 3, 4, & 5. Making Specific Gifts

You'll recall that in Chapter 5 you provided a detailed description of all your property. Then, in Chapter 6, you divided up this property by selecting the beneficiaries you want to inherit specific items as well as your residuary estate. Finally, you selected alternate beneficiaries to take your gifts in case your primary beneficiaries fail to survive you by the period specified in your will, which is 45 days in all Chapter 11 basic wills. Now you need to transfer the information from

Chapters 5 and 6 to the appropriate location in the basic will you have selected. To do this, do the following:

To Complete Clause 3: Transfer each cash gift from the Beneficiary Chart in Chapter 6 to Clause 3. Then, fill in the names of the primary and alternate beneficiaries who you designated in Chapter 6 to receive these cash gifts. Here is what Clause 3 looks like:

3. I make the following cash gifts:

I give _____ $10,000 _____

to _____ Rudolph Phelps _____ or, if

_____ he _____ does not

survive me by 45 days, to _____ Andrew Phelps _____.

To Complete Clause 4: Transfer each personal property gift (other than cash) listed in Chapter 6 to Clause 4. For your description of each gift, use the one you prepared in the chart in Chapter 5.[2]

Then, fill in the names of the primary and alternate beneficiaries who you designated in Chapter 6 to receive these personal property items. Here is an example of Clause 4:

4. I make the following specific gifts of personal property:

I give _____ all my stocks _____

_____

to _____ my mate Ellen Zywansky _____ or, if

_____ she _____ does not

survive me by 45 days, to _____ my brother Ted O'Connor _____.

Note: It is perfectly okay to give a number of personal property items in one blank (e.g., "I give my gold watch, skis, and coin collection to Wilfred Brown...").

To Complete Clause 5: Transfer each real property gift listed in Chapter 6 to Clause 5. Use the description for this property which you prepared in Chapter 5.[3]

Here is what Clause 5. looks like.

5. I make the following specific gifts of real property:

I give the property commonly known as _____ my condominium apartment
_____ at 2 Park Ave., New York, New York _____

to _____ my wife Rose Elliot _____ or, if

---

[2] If you skipped the property inventory chart in chapter 5 because of the simple way you plan to leave your property, review our instructions in that chapter for making property descriptions before filling out the will clauses in this chapter.

[3] See the previous footnote

_____she_____ does not

survive me by 45 days, to _my children Roger and_
Susan Elliot, in equal shares .

I give the property commonly known as _my interest in_
the B-Bar Ranch, Alamos, Texas
to _my grandson, Theodore Taft Elliot_ or, if
_____he_____ does not

survive me by 45 days, to _my best friend Michael L. Smith_ .

That's all there is to it. If you run out of room in Clauses 3, 4 or 5, simply prepare an attachment the way we suggested at the beginning of this chapter.

Clause 6. The "Residue" of Your Estate

As you know by now, the "residue" of your estate is exactly what it sounds like—all that remains after all specific gifts have been distributed. You named a residuary beneficiary and alternate residuary beneficiary in the chart in Chapter 6. Here is the residuary clause:

6. I give my residuary estate, i.e., the rest of my property not otherwise specifically and validly disposed of by this will or in any other manner, to _my husband_
Tom Harras or if _he_ fails to survive me by 45 days, to
my child Linda Harras Smith .

Note: In addition to providing for your primary and alternate residuary beneficiaries, the residuary clause also provides that:

• Specific gifts shall pass into your residuary estate in the event all the primary and alternate beneficiaries you name to receive the gift fail to survive you by 45 days; and

• Alternate beneficiaries of shared gifts of all types (including shared residuary gifts) only take the gift if all the primary beneficiaries fail to survive you by 45 days.

Warning: Here's one last reminder to be sure you've given something to each of your children (and children of a deceased child) in your will. Otherwise, you will need to use a Chapter 12 will to disinherit a child or children.

Also Important: The form wills provide that all your debts and taxes are paid first from your residuary estate. This is the way most people do it. If you want a different arrangement, however, use Chapter 12 to construct your will.

Clause 7. Name Your Executor

Here you name your executor and successor executor, the people you chose in Chapter 3 to be responsible for supervising the distribution of your property. Here is what the clause looks like:

7. I nominate _Mary O'Railley_ as executor to serve without bond. If _Mary O'Railley_ shall for any reason fail to qualify or cease to act as executor, I nominate _____ _Tom O'Railley_, also to serve without bond.

Clause 8.   Simultaneous Death Clause (for those with a spouse or mate)

Note: The sample clause below assumes a married woman is making a will. A husband would obviously complete this clause by filling in his wife's name, or simply by using the word "wife" in the appropriate blank.

8. If _my husband_ and I should die simultaneously,
wife/husband

or under such circumstances as to render it difficult or impossible to determine by clear

and convincing evidence who predeceased the other, I shall be conclusively presumed

to have survived _my husband_ for purposes of this will.
wife/husband

Clause 9. Name a Guardian of a Minor's Person and Property

If you have minor children, you should use basic will form II, IV or VI, depending upon your marital/mate status. Each of these will forms contains provisions for you to (1) suggest a personal guardian for your minor children if there is no living person entitled to legal custody who is available to assume it, and (2) appoint their property guardian. (See Chapter 7, Sections B and C.)

9. If at my death any of my children are minors and a guardian is needed, I recommend that ___*Ruby Johnson*___, be appointed guardian of the
name

person(s) of my minor children. If ___*Ruby Johnson*___ cannot
name

serve as personal guardian, I recommend that ___*Fran Johnson*___,
name

be appointed personal guardian.

I appoint ___*Ruby Johnson*___ as the property guardian of
name

my minor children. If ___*Ruby Johnson*___ cannot serve as
name

property guardian, I appoint ___*Fran Johnson*___ as property
name

guardian.

I direct no bond be required of any guardian.

If you want to state reasons in your will why the person you name is the most desirable guardian for your children (see Chapter 7, Section B), or if you want to appoint different guardians for different children, you'll need to use Chapter 12 to draft your will.

Clause 10.   Establish a Trust for Property Left to Minor Children

The basic wills allow you to leave property to one or more of your minor children in separate trusts. This option is especially advised for any minor child to whom you plan to leave property valued in excess of $25,000 (see discussion in Chapter 7, Section C) if you do not want the child to take title to the property at age 18.

By using a trust, you can determine an age between 18 to 30 when the trust shall end. If you fail to specify an age, the trust automatically terminates when the child becomes 30.[4] When the

---

4 ▲ There is nothing to legally stop you from choosing an older age than 30 to designate the age at which the trust ends and the beneficiary gets the property. However, I strongly suggest that you not list an older age unless you consult with a lawyer. My reason is that while the sort of simple trust I include here is well-suited to delay the age at which a child takes property for a few years it is less appropriate to provide for the lifetime management of money, particularly for an incapacitated or improvident person.

trust option is selected for a minor child, all property left to that child is placed in a separate trust to be managed by the trustee for the benefit of the child.

10. All property I give in this will to any of the children listed in Section A below who are minors at my death shall be held for each of them in a separate trust, pursuant to the following trust terms, which shall apply to each trust:

A. Trust Beneficiaries and Age Limits

Each trust shall end when the following beneficiaries become 30, except as otherwise specified:

Trust for	Shall end at age
my son Jaime	28
my daughter Juanita	24
my son Pedro	28

After you've completed the age provision for the children's trust, you next complete the provision appointing a trustee to manage the trust or trusts. Here is what the provision looks like:

The trustee shall be ___Ruby Johnson___, or, if

___Ruby Johnson___ cannot serve as trustee, the
        name

trustee shall be ___Fran Johnson___. No bond
        name

shall be required of any named trustee.

Note: Do not appoint more than one trustee or one successor trustee.

Signature Clause

I show you how to sign your will and have it witnessed in Chapter 13. In addition, if you decide to make your will self-proving, follow the instructions in Chapter 13.

D. Making Changes in a Basic Will

As has been emphasized, making any changes in a basic will form other than simple common sense ones such as adjusting tenses and pronouns is discouraged. The purpose of a basic will is to provide clarity and simplicity. Making changes risks confusion and potential ineffectiveness.

E. Sample Completed Basic Will

Before filling in your basic will, it should be helpful to see what a filled-in one looks like. For this reason I provide the following example. Examining it with care will reassure you that it really isn't hard to do your own will.

Mark and Linda are married, in their 30's, with two young children. Mark is employed as an accountant. Linda works part-time as a proofreader for a publisher. They live in a community property state and own their house (heavily mortgaged) "as community property." (In a common law state, they would also each own one-half of the house, since they listed both names on the deed.) This is their major asset. They also own, as community property, two cars, an old Ford convertible and a Toyota station wagon, the furnishings of their home, personal possessions like clothing, tools stereos, etc., $6,000 in a savings account in Mark's name, and $8,000 each in IRAs.

Mark and Linda each want to leave their entire estate to the other, except that Mark wants to give his tools to his brother, his Ford convertible to a friend, and $5,000 to his sister.[5] In determining their estate plan, they decide they need to purchase substantial amounts of insurance

---

[5]These items are community property, so Mark legally can only give his one-half interest in them by his will--unless Mark's wife agrees, in writing, to allow him to give away her half interest. In a common law state, Mark could give $6,000 from the savings account (since it's in his name) and the tools if he purchased them.

on both their lives to protect their children. They each purchase $100,000 worth of term life insurance. Each names the other as beneficiary of their IRA. Then each prepares a will, using form IV (will for a husband or wife with minor children).

Here is Mark's will draft. Note that Mark does not sign his will yet, as it hasn't been typed.

WILL OF _____*Mark P. Creery*_____.
your name

I,_____*Mark P. Creery*_____, a resident of
your name

_____*Hayward*_____, _____*Alameda County*_____,
city   county

_____*California*_____ declare that this is my will.
state

1. I revoke all wills and codicils that I have previously made.

2. I am married to _____*Linda F. Creery*_____, and all references in this will to my ___*wife*___ are to ___*her*___. I was
husband/wife   him/her

previously married to _____. That marriage was terminated by _____.

I am the ___*father*___ of the following children, whose names and dates of
father/mother

birth are:

_____*Anthony A. Creery*_____   ___*10/12/83*___
Name   Date of Birth

_____*Jennifer S. Creery*_____   ___*11/7/85*___
Name   Date of Birth

_____   _____
Name   Date of Birth

_____   _____
Name   Date of Birth

There are _____ living children of my deceased child _____:

_____   _____
Name of Grandchild   Date of Birth

_____   _____
Name of Grandchild   Date of Birth

_____   _____
Name of Grandchild   Date of Birth

(repeat as needed)

3. I make the following cash gifts:

I give ___$5000_____

to _my sister Mary Creery Noonan_____ or, if

_____she_____ does not

survive me by 45 days, to _her children in equal shares_.

I give _____

to _____ or, if

_____ does not

survive me by 45 days, to _____

I give _____

to _____ or, if

_____ does not

survive me by 45 days, to _____

I give _____

to _____ or, if

_____ does not

survive me by 45 days, to _____

I give _____

to _____ or, if

_____ does not

survive me by 45 days, to _____

I give _____

to _____ or, if

_____ does not

survive me by 45 days, to _____

4. I make the following specific gifts of personal property:

I give ___my power tools_____

_____

to _my brother John Creery_ _____ or, if
_____ _he_ _____ does not
survive me by 45 days, to _my wife_ _____.

I give _my 1950 Ford convertible_ _____
_____

to _my best friend Ray Ellington_ _____ or, if
_____ _he_ _____ does not
survive me by 45 days, to _my wife_ _____.

I give _____
_____

to _____ or, if
_____ does not
survive me by 45 days, to _____

I give _____
_____

to _____ or, if
_____ does not
survive me by 45 days, to _____

I give _____
_____

to _____ or, if
_____ does not
survive me by 45 days, to _____

I give _____
_____

to _____ or, if
_____ does not
survive me by 45 days, to _____

I give _____

_____

to _____ or, if

_____ does not

survive me by 45 days, to _____

5. I make the following specific gifts of real property:

I give the property commonly known as *my share of 107*
Dream Ave., Hayward
to *my wife* _____ or, if
she _____ does not
survive me by 45 days, to *my children in equal shares* .

I give the property commonly known as_____

_____

to _____ or, if

_____ does not

survive me by 45 days, to _____.

I give the property commonly known as_____

_____

to _____ or, if

_____ does not

survive me by 45 days, to _____.

I give the property commonly known as_____

_____

to _____ or, if

_____ does not

survive me by 45 days, to _____.

6. I give my residuary estate, i.e., the rest of my property not otherwise specifically and
validly disposed of by this will or in any other manner, to *my wife*
Linda , or, if *she* fails to survive me by 45 days, to
my children in equal shares .

If any primary beneficiary of a shared residuary or specific gift made in this will fails to

survive me by 45 days, the surviving beneficiaries of that gift shall equally divide that deceased beneficiary's share. If all primary beneficiaries of a shared residuary or specific gift fail to survive me by 45 days, that gift shall pass to the named alternate beneficiaries for that gift, in equal shares. If the alternate beneficiaries named by this will to receive a specific gift do not survive me by 45 days, or there are no such named alternate bene-ficiaries, that gift shall become part of my residuary estate.

7. I nominate _Linda F. Creery_ as executor, to serve without bond. If _she_ shall for any reason fail to qualify or cease to act as executor, I nominate _John Creery_, also to serve without bond. I direct that my executor take all actions legally permissible to have the probate of my estate done as simply as possible, including filing a petition in the appropriate court for the independent administration of my estate.

[To save space, I do not repeat the lengthy executor's powers provision from the box on page 11:55 now. Mr. Creery would insert this material here.]

8. If my _wife_ and I should die simultaneously or under such
wife/husband
circumstances as to render it difficult or impossible to determine by clear and convincing evidence who predeceased the other, I shall be conclusively presumed to have survived my _wife_ for purposes of this will.
wife/husband

9. If at my death any of my children are minors and a guardian is needed, I recommend that _my wife's sister Joan Roy_ be appointed as guardian of the
name
person(s) of my minor children. If _Joan Roy_ cannot
name
serve as personal guardian, I recommend that _Mary Roy_
name
be appointed personal guardian.

I appoint _Joan Roy_ as property guardian of my minor
name
children. If _Joan Roy_ cannot serve as property guardian, I
name
appoint _Mary Roy_ as property guardian.
name

I direct that no bond be required of any guardian.

10. All property I give in this will to any of the children listed in Section A below who are minors at my death shall be held for each of them in a separate trust, pursuant to the following trust terms, which shall apply to each trust:

A. Trust Beneficiaries and Age Limits

Each trust shall end when the following beneficiaries become 30, except as otherwise specified:

Trust for	Shall end at age
Anthony A. Creery	25
Jennifer S. Creery	25

B. Trustees

The trustee shall be _____ Joan Roy _____, or, if _she_ cannot serve as trustee, the trustee shall be ___ Mary Roy ___.
No bond shall be required of any trustee.

[Insert trust provisions contained in box on page 11:56-57.]

[To save space I do not repeat the lengthy trust provisions now. Mr. Creery would insert this material here.]

I subscribe my name to this will this _____ day of _____, 19___, at _____, _____,
     city   county
_____, and do hereby declare that I sign and execute
     state
this instrument as my last will and that I sign it willingly, that I execute it as my free and voluntary act for the purposes therein expressed, and that I am of the age of majority or otherwise legally empowered to make a will, and under no constraint or undue influence.

_____
your signed name

On this _____ day of _____, 19__,

_____*Mark P. Creery*_____ declared to us, the undersigned, that
　　　　　　　your name

this instrument was _____*his*_____ will and requested us to act as witnesses to it.
　　　　　　　　　　　　his/her

____*He*____ thereupon signed this will in our presence, all of us being present
　　He/She

at the same time. We now, at _____*his*_____ request, in _____*his*_____
　　　　　　　　　　　　　　　　his/her　　　　　　　　　*his/her*

presence, and in the presence of each other, subscribe our names as witnesses and

declare we understand this to be _____*his*_____ will, and that to the best of our
　　　　　　　　　　　　　　　　　　　his/her

knowledge the testator is of the age of majority, or is otherwise legally empowered to

make a will, and under no constraint or undue influence.

　　We declare under penalty of perjury that the foregoing is true and correct.

_____ residing at _____

　　　　　　　　　　　　　　　　　　　　　 _____

_____ residing at _____

　　　　　　　　　　　　　　　　　　　　　 _____

_____ residing at _____

　　　　　　　　　　　　　　　　　　　　　 _____

F. Basic Will Forms

　　Now it's time to actually fill in the information necessary to make your will. Again, there are six wills set out here as follows:

　　I. Will for a single person with no minor children

　　II. Will for a single person with minor children

　　III. Will for a husband or wife with no minor children

　　IV. Will for a husband or wife with minor children

　　V. Will for a person who lives with a lover/mate and who has no minor children

　　VI. Will for a person who lives with a lover/mate and who has minor children

　　Select the one that applies to you and prepare it following the instructions set out in Section B above.

I. Will for a Single Person With No Minor Children

WILL OF _____.

your name

I, _____, a resident of

your name

_____, _____,

city   county

_____ declare that this is my will.

state

1. I revoke all wills and codicils that I have previously made.

2. I am not married.

[If appropriate, complete:

I was previously married to _____. That marriage was

terminated by _____.

I am the _____ of the following adult children whose names and dates

mother/father

of birth are:

_____   _____

Name   Date of Birth

_____   _____

Name   Date of Birth

_____   _____

Name   Date of Birth

_____   _____

Name   Date of Birth

_____   _____

Name   Date of Birth

There are _____ living children of my deceased child _____:

_____   _____

Name of Grandchild   Date of Birth

_____   _____

Name of Grandchild   Date of Birth

_____   _____]

Name of Grandchild   Date of Birth

[repeat as needed]

I give _____

to _____ or, if

_____ does not

survive me by 45 days, to _____.

I give _____

to _____ or, if

_____ does not

survive me by 45 days, to _____.

I give _____

to _____ or, if

_____ does not

survive me by 45 days, to _____.

I give _____

to _____ or, if

_____ does not

survive me by 45 days, to _____.

I give _____

to _____ or, if

_____ does not

survive me by 45 days, to _____.

I give _____

to _____ or, if

_____ does not

survive me by 45 days, to _____.

4. I make the following specific gifts of personal property:

I give _____

_____

to _____ or, if

_____ does not

survive me by 45 days, to _____.

I give _____

_____

to _____ or, if

_____ does not

survive me by 45 days, to _____.

   I give _____

_____

to _____ or, if

_____ does not

survive me by 45 days, to _____.

   I give _____

_____

to _____ or, if

_____ does not

survive me by 45 days, to _____.

   I give _____

_____

to _____ or, if

_____ does not

survive me by 45 days, to _____.

   I give _____

_____

to _____ or, if

_____ does not

survive me by 45 days, to _____.

   5. I make the following specific gifts of real property:

   I give the property commonly known as_____

_____

to _____ or, if

_____ does not

survive me by 45 days, to _____.

   I give the property commonly known as_____

_____

to _____ or, if

_____ does not

survive me by 45 days, to _____.

   I give the property commonly known as_____

_____

to _____ or, if

_____ does not

survive me by 45 days, to _____.

   I give the property commonly known as_____

_____

to _____ or, if

_____ does not

survive me by 45 days, to _____.

   6. I give my residuary estate, i.e., the rest of my property not otherwise specifically and
validly disposed of by this will or in any other manner,

to_____, or, if

_____ fails to survive me by 45 days, to _____

_____.

   If any primary beneficiary of a shared residuary or specific gift made in this will fails to
survive me by 45 days, the surviving beneficiaries of that gift shall equally divide the
deceased beneficiary's share. If all primary beneficiaries of a shared residuary or specific
gift fail to survive me by 45 days, that gift shall pass in equal shares to the alternate
beneficiaries named to receive that gift. If the alternate beneficiaries named by this will to
receive a specific gift do not survive me by 45 days, or there are no such named alternate
beneficiaries, that gift shall become part of my residuary estate.

   7. I nominate _____ as executor, to serve
without bond. If _____ shall for any reason fail to
qualify or cease to act as executor, I nominate _____ as
executor, also to serve without bond. I direct that my executor take all actions legally
permissible to have the probate of my estate done as simply as possible, including filing a
petition in the appropriate court for the independent administration of my estate.

   [Insert executor's powers contained in box on page 11:55 here.]

I subscribe my name to this will this _____ day of _____,
19___, at _____, _____,
city   county

_____, and do hereby declare that I sign and execute
state
this instrument as my last will and that I sign it willingly, that I execute it as my free and
voluntary act for the purposes therein expressed, and that I am of the age of majority or
otherwise legally empowered to make a will, and under no constraint or undue influence.

_____
your signed name

On this _____ day of _____, 19__,

_____ declared to us, the undersigned, that
your name

this instrument was _____ will and requested us to act as witnesses to it.
his/her

_____ thereupon signed this will in our presence, all of us being present
He/She

at the same time. We now, at _____ request, in _____
his/her   his/her

presence, and in the presence of each other, subscribe our names as witnesses and

declare we understand this to be _____ will, and that to the best of our
his/her

knowledge the testator is of the age of majority, or is otherwise legally empowered to

make a will, and under no constraint or undue influence.

We declare under penalty of perjury that the foregoing is true and correct.

_____ residing at _____

_____

_____ residing at _____

_____

_____ residing at _____

_____

II. Will for a Single Person with Minor Children

WILL OF _____.
　　　　　　　　　　　　　　　your name

I, _____, a resident of
　　　　　　　　　　your name

_____, _____,
　　　　　city　　　　　　　　　　　　county

_____ declare that this is my will.
　　　　state

　　1. I revoke all wills and codicils that I have previously made.

　　2. I am not married.

[If appropriate, complete:

　　I was previously married to _____.

That marriage was terminated by _____.

　　I am the _____ of _____ children whose names and dates of birth are:
　　　　　　　mother/father

_____　　　_____
Name　　　　　　　　　　　　　　　　　　　　　Date of Birth

_____　　　_____
Name　　　　　　　　　　　　　　　　　　　　　Date of Birth

_____　　　_____
Name　　　　　　　　　　　　　　　　　　　　　Date of Birth

_____　　　_____
Name　　　　　　　　　　　　　　　　　　　　　Date of Birth

_____　　　_____
Name　　　　　　　　　　　　　　　　　　　　　Date of Birth

　　There are _____ living children of my deceased child _____:

_____　　　_____
Name of Grandchild　　　　　　　　　　　　　　Date of Birth

_____　　　_____
Name of Grandchild　　　　　　　　　　　　　　Date of Birth

_____　　　_____]
Name of Grandchild　　　　　　　　　　　　　　Date of Birth

[repeat as needed]

3. I give the following cash gifts:

I give _____

to _____ or, if

_____ does not

survive me by 45 days, to _____.

I give _____

to _____ or, if

_____ does not

survive me by 45 days, to _____.

I give _____

to _____ or, if

_____ does not

survive me by 45 days, to _____.

I give _____

to _____ or, if

_____ does not

survive me by 45 days, to _____.

I give _____

to _____ or, if

_____ does not

survive me by 45 days, to _____.

I give _____

to _____ or, if

_____ does not

survive me by 45 days, to _____.

4. I make the following specific gifts of personal property:

I give _____

_____

to _____ or, if

_____ does not

survive me by 45 days, to _____.

I give _____

_____

to _____ or, if

_____ does not

survive me by 45 days, to _____.

I give _____

_____

to _____ or, if

_____ does not

survive me by 45 days, to _____.

I give _____

_____

to _____ or, if

_____ does not

survive me by 45 days, to _____.

I give _____

_____

to _____ or, if

_____ does not

survive me by 45 days, to _____.

I give _____

_____

to _____ or, if

_____ does not

survive me by 45 days, to _____.

5. I make the following specific gifts of real property:

I give the property commonly known as_____

_____

to _____ or, if

_____ does not

survive me by 45 days, to _____.

I give the property commonly known as_____

_____

to _____ or, if

_____ does not

survive me by 45 days, to _____.

I give the property commonly known as_____

_____

to _____ or, if

_____ does not

survive me by 45 days, to _____.

I give the property commonly known as_____

_____

to _____ or, if

_____ does not

survive me by 45 days, to _____.

6. I give my residuary estate, i.e., the rest of my property not otherwise specifically and validly disposed of by this will or in any other manner, to _____ or if _____ fails to survive me by 45 days, to

_____.

If any primary beneficiary of a shared residuary or specific gift made in this will fails to survive me by 45 days, the surviving beneficiaries of that gift shall equally divide the deceased beneficiary's share. If all primary beneficiaries of a shared residuary or specific gift fail to survive me by 45 days, that gift shall pass in equal shares to the alternate beneficiaries named to receive that gift. If the alternate beneficiaries named by this will to receive a specific gift do not survive me by 45 days, or there are no such named alternate beneficiaries, that gift shall become part of my residuary estate.

7. I nominate _____ as executor of this will, to serve without bond. If _____ shall for any reason fail to qualify or cease to act as executor, I nominate _____ as executor, also to serve without bond. I direct that my executor take all actions legally permissible to

have the probate of my estate done as simply as possible, including filing a petition in the appropriate court for the independent administration of my estate.

[Insert executor's powers from box on page 11:55 here.]

8. If at my death any of my children are minors, and a guardian is needed, I recommend that _____ be appointed guardian of the person(s) of

name
my minor children. If _____ cannot serve as personal

name
guardian, I recommend that _____ be appointed

name
personal guardian.

I appoint _____ as the guardian of the property of my minor children. If _____ cannot serve as property guardian, I appoint _____ as property guardian.

I direct no bond be required of any guardian.

9. All property I give in this will to any of the children listed in Section A below who are minors at my death shall be held for each of them in a separate trust, pursuant to the following trust terms, which shall apply to each trust:

A. Trust Beneficiaries and Age Limits

Each trust shall end when the following beneficiaries become 30, except as otherwise specified in this section:

Trust for	Shall end at age
_____	_____
_____	_____
_____	_____
_____	_____
_____	_____

B. Trustees

The trustee shall be _____, or, if

_____ cannot serve as trustee, the trustee shall be

_____. No bond shall be required of any trustee.

[Insert trust provisions contained in box on page 11:56-57.]

I subscribe my name to this will this _____ day of _____,

19____, at _____, _____,
                        city   county

_____, and do hereby declare that I sign and execute
                      state

this instrument as my last will and that I sign it willingly, that I execute it as my free and

voluntary act for the purposes therein expressed, and that I am of the age of majority or

otherwise legally empowered to make a will, and under no constraint or undue influence.

_____
                      your signed name

On this _____ day of _____, 19___,

_____ declared to us, the undersigned, that
                      your name

this instrument was _____ will and requested us to act as witnesses to it.
                            his/her

_____ thereupon signed this will in our presence, all of us being present
        He/She

at the same time. We now, at _____ request, in _____
                                          his/her   his/her

presence, and in the presence of each other, subscribe our names as witnesses and

declare we understand this to be _____ will, and that to the best of our
                                              his/her

knowledge the testator is of the age of majority, or is otherwise legally empowered to

make a will, and under no constraint or undue influence.

We declare under penalty of perjury that the foregoing is true and correct.

_____ residing at _____

_____

_____ residing at _____

_____

_____ residing at _____

_____

III. Will for a Husband or Wife with No Minor Children

WILL OF _____.
your name

I, _____, a resident of
your name

_____, _____,
city   county

_____ declare that this is my will.
state

1. I revoke all wills and codicils that I have previously made.

2. I am married to _____, and all

references in this will to my _____ are to _____. I was
husband/wife   him/her

previously married to _____. That marriage was terminated

by _____.

   I am the _____ of the following children, whose names and dates
father/mother

of birth are:

_____   _____
Name   Date of Birth

_____   _____
Name   Date of Birth

_____   _____
Name   Date of Birth

_____   _____
Name   Date of Birth

   There are _____ living children of my deceased child _____:

_____   _____
Name of Grandchild   Date of Birth

_____   _____
Name of Grandchild   Date of Birth

_____   _____
Name of Grandchild   Date of Birth

(repeat as needed)

3. I make the following cash gifts:

I give _____

to _____ or, if

_____ does not

survive me by 45 days, to _____.

I give _____

to _____ or, if

_____ does not

survive me by 45 days, to _____.

I give _____

to _____ or, if

_____ does not

survive me by 45 days, to _____.

I give _____

to _____ or, if

_____ does not

survive me by 45 days, to _____.

I give _____

to _____ or, if

_____ does not

survive me by 45 days, to _____.

I give _____

to _____ or, if

_____ does not

survive me by 45 days, to _____.

4. I make the following specific gifts of personal property:

I give _____

_____

to _____ or, if

_____ does not

survive me by 45 days, to _____.

I give _____

_____

to _____ or, if

_____ does not

survive me by 45 days, to _____.

I give _____

_____

to _____ or, if

_____ does not

survive me by 45 days, to _____.

I give _____

_____

to _____ or, if

_____ does not

survive me by 45 days, to _____.

I give _____

_____

to _____ or, if

_____ does not

survive me by 45 days, to _____.

I give _____

_____

to _____ or, if

_____ does not

survive me by 45 days, to _____.

5. I make the following specific gifts of real property:

I give the property commonly known as_____

_____

to _____ or, if

_____ does not

survive me by 45 days, to _____.

I give the property commonly known as_____

_____

to _____ or, if

_____ does not

survive me by 45 days, to _____.

I give the property commonly known as_____

_____

to _____ or, if

_____ does not

survive me by 45 days, to _____.

I give the property commonly known as_____

_____

to _____ or, if

_____ does not

survive me by 45 days, to _____.

6. I give my residuary estate, i.e., the rest of my property not otherwise specifically and validly disposed of by this will or in any other manner, to _____ or if _____ fails to survive me by 45 days, to

_____.

If any primary beneficiary of a shared residuary or specific gift made in this will fails to survive me by 45 days, the surviving beneficiaries of that gift shall equally divide the deceased beneficiary's share. If all primary beneficiaries of a shared residuary or specific gift fail to survive me by 45 days, that gift shall pass in equal shares to the alternate beneficiaries named to receive that gift. If the alternate beneficiaries named by this will to receive a specific gift do not survive me by 45 days, or there are no such named alternate beneficiaries, that gift shall become part of my residuary estate.

7. I nominate _____ as executor, to serve without bond. If _____ shall for any reason fail to qualify or cease to act as executor, I nominate _____ as executor, also to serve without bond. I direct that my executor take all actions legally

permissible to have the probate of my estate done as simply as possible, including filing a petition in the appropriate court for the independent administration of my estate.

[Insert executor's powers contained in box on page 11:55 here.]

8. If my _____ and I should die simultaneously, or under such circumstances
          wife/husband

as to render it difficult or impossible to determine by clear and convincing evidence who predeceased the other, I shall be conclusively presumed to have survived my

_____ for purposes of this will.
wife/husband

I subscribe my name to this will this _____ day of _____,

19___, at _____, _____,
                        city   county

_____, and do hereby declare that I sign and execute
            state

this instrument as my last will and that I sign it willingly, that I execute it as my free and voluntary act for the purposes therein expressed, and that I am of the age of majority or otherwise legally empowered to make a will, and under no constraint or undue influence.

_____
              your signed name

On this _____ day of _____, 19__,

_____ declared to us, the undersigned, that
                    your name

this instrument was _____ will and requested us to act as witnesses to it.
                              his/her

_____ thereupon signed this will in our presence, all of us being present
  He/She

at the same time. We now, at _____ request, in _____
                                          his/her   his/her

presence, and in the presence of each other, subscribe our names as witnesses and declare we understand this to be _____ will, and that to the best of our
                                              his/her

knowledge the testator is of the age of majority, or is otherwise legally empowered to make a will, and under no constraint or undue influence.

We declare under penalty of perjury that the foregoing is true and correct.

_____ residing at _____

_____

_____   residing at _____

_____

_____   residing at _____

_____

IV. Will for a Husband or Wife with Minor Children

WILL OF _____.
your name

I, _____, a resident of
your name

_____, _____,
city   county

_____ declare that this is my will.
state

1. I revoke all wills and codicils that I have previously made.

2. I am married to _____, and
all references in this will to my _____ are to _____. I was
husband/wife   him/her
previously married to _____. That marriage was terminated
by _____.

I am the _____ of the following children, whose names and dates
father/mother
of birth are:

_____   _____
Name   Date of Birth

_____   _____
Name   Date of Birth

_____   _____
Name   Date of Birth

_____   _____
Name   Date of Birth

There are _____ living children of my deceased child _____:

_____   _____
Name of Grandchild   Date of Birth

_____   _____
Name of Grandchild   Date of Birth

_____   _____
Name of Grandchild   Date of Birth

(repeat as needed)

3. I make the following cash gifts:

I give _____

to _____ or, if

_____ does not

survive me by 45 days, to _____.

I give _____

to _____ or, if

_____ does not

survive me by 45 days, to _____.

I give _____

to _____ or, if

_____ does not

survive me by 45 days, to _____.

I give _____

to _____ or, if

_____ does not

survive me by 45 days, to _____.

I give _____

to _____ or, if

_____ does not

survive me by 45 days, to _____.

I give _____

to _____ or, if

_____ does not

survive me by 45 days, to _____.

4. I make the following specific gifts of personal property:

I give _____

_____

to _____ or, if

_____ does not

survive me by 45 days, to _____.

I give _____

_____

to _____ or, if

_____ does not

survive me by 45 days, to _____.

I give _____

_____

to _____ or, if

_____ does not

survive me by 45 days, to _____.

I give _____

_____

to _____ or, if

_____ does not

survive me by 45 days, to _____.

I give _____

_____

to _____ or, if

_____ does not

survive me by 45 days, to _____.

I give _____

_____

to _____ or, if

_____ does not

survive me by 45 days, to _____.

5. I make the following specific gifts of real property:

I give the property commonly known as_____

_____

to _____ or, if

_____ does not

survive me by 45 days, to _____.

I give the property commonly known as_____

_____

to _____ or, if

_____ does not

survive me by 45 days, to _____.

I give the property commonly known as_____

_____

to _____ or, if

_____ does not

survive me by 45 days, to _____.

I give the property commonly known as_____

_____

to _____ or, if

_____ does not

survive me by 45 days, to _____.

6. I give my residuary estate, i.e., the rest of my property not otherwise specifically and validly disposed of by this will or in any other manner, to _____ or if _____ fails to survive me by 45 days, to

_____.

If any primary beneficiary of a shared residuary or specific gift made in this will fails to survive me by 45 days, the surviving beneficiaries of that gift shall equally divide the deceased beneficiary's share. If all primary beneficiaries of a shared residuary or specific gift fail to survive me by 45 days, that gift shall pass in equal shares to the alternate beneficiaries named to receive that gift. If the alternate beneficiaries named by this will to receive a specific gift do not survive me by 45 days, or there are no such named alternate beneficiaries, that gift shall become part of my residuary estate.

7. I nominate _____ as executor, to serve without bond. If _____ shall for any reason fail to qualify or cease to act as executor, I nominate _____ as executor, also to serve without bond. I direct that my executor take all actions legally permissible to

have the probate of my estate done as simply as possible, including filing a petition in the appropriate court for the independent administration of my estate.

[Insert executor's powers contained in box on page 11:55.]

8. If my _____ and I should die simultaneously, or under such circumstances
        wife/husband
as to render it difficult or impossible to determine by clear and convincing evidence who predeceased the other, I shall be conclusively presumed to have survived my

_____ for purposes of this will.
wife/husband

9. If at my death any of my children are minors, and a guardian is needed, I recommend that _____ be appointed guardian of the person(s) of
                        name
my minor children. If _____ cannot serve as personal
                                name
guardian, I recommend that _____ be appointed
                                        name
personal guardian.

I appoint _____ as property guardian of my minor
                        name
children. If _____ cannot serve as property guardian, I
                    name
appoint _____ as property guardian.
                    name

I direct no bond be required of any guardian.

10. All property I give in this will to any of the children listed in Section A below who are minors at my death shall be held for each of them in a separate trust, pursuant to the following trust terms, which shall apply to each trust:

A. Trust Beneficiaries and Age Limits

Each trust shall end when the following beneficiaries become 30, except as otherwise specified in this section:

Trust for	Shall end at age
_____	_____
_____	_____
_____	_____
_____	_____
_____	_____

B. Trustees

The trustee shall be _____, or, if

_____ cannot serve as trustee, the trustee shall be

_____. No bond shall be required of any trustee.

[Insert trust provisions contained in box on page 11:56-57.]

I subscribe my name to this will this _____ day of _____,

19___, at _____, _____,
                          city   county

_____, and do hereby declare that I sign and execute
              state

this instrument as my last will and that I sign it willingly, that I execute it as my free and

voluntary act for the purposes therein expressed, and that I am of the age of majority or

otherwise legally empowered to make a will, and under no constraint or undue influence.

_____
              your signed name

On this _____ day of _____, 19__,

_____ declared to us, the undersigned, that
              your name

this instrument was _____ will and requested us to act as witnesses to it.
                          his/her

_____ thereupon signed this will in our presence, all of us being present
    He/She

at the same time. We now, at _____ request, in _____
                                        his/her   his/her

presence, and in the presence of each other, subscribe our names as witnesses and

declare we understand this to be _____ will, and that to the best of our
                                          his/her

knowledge the testator is of the age of majority, or is otherwise legally empowered to

make a will, and under no constraint or undue influence.

We declare under penalty of perjury that the foregoing is true and correct.

_____ residing at _____

_____

_____ residing at _____

_____

_____ residing at _____

_____

V. Will for a Person Who Lives with a Lover/Mate and Who Has No Minor Children

WILL OF _____.
your name

I, _____, a resident of
your name

_____, _____,
city   county

_____ declare that this is my will.
state

1. I revoke all wills and codicils that I have previously made.

2. My _____ name is _____, and all
lover/mate's

references in this will to my _____ are to _____.
lover/mate   him/her

[If appropriate, complete:

I was previously married to _____. That marriage was

terminated by _____.

I am the _____ of the following children, whose names and
father/mother

dates of birth are:

_____   _____
Name   Date of Birth

_____   _____
Name   Date of Birth

_____   _____
Name   Date of Birth

_____   _____
Name   Date of Birth

There are ____ living children of my deceased child _____:

_____   _____
Name   Date of Birth

_____   _____
Name   Date of Birth

_____   _____]
Name   Date of Birth

(repeat as needed)

3. I make the following cash gifts:

I give _____

to _____ or, if

_____ does not

survive me by 45 days, to _____.

I give _____

to _____ or, if

_____ does not

survive me by 45 days, to _____.

I give _____

to _____ or, if

_____ does not

survive me by 45 days, to _____.

I give _____

to _____ or, if

_____ does not

survive me by 45 days, to _____.

I give _____

to _____ or, if

_____ does not

survive me by 45 days, to _____.

I give _____

to _____ or, if

_____ does not

survive me by 45 days, to _____.

4. I make the following specific gifts of personal property:

I give _____

_____

to _____ or, if

_____ does not

survive me by 45 days, to _____.

I give _____

_____

to _____ or, if

_____ does not

survive me by 45 days, to _____.

I give _____

_____

to _____ or, if

_____ does not

survive me by 45 days, to _____.

I give _____

_____

to _____ or, if

_____ does not

survive me by 45 days, to _____.

I give _____

_____

to _____ or, if

_____ does not

survive me by 45 days, to _____.

I give _____

_____

to _____ or, if

_____ does not

survive me by 45 days, to _____.

5. I make the following specific gifts of real property:

I give the property commonly known as_____

_____

to _____ or, if

_____ does not

survive me by 45 days, to _____.

I give the property commonly known as_____

_____

to _____ or, if

_____ does not

survive me by 45 days, to _____.

I give the property commonly known as_____

_____

to _____ or, if

_____ does not

survive me by 45 days, to _____.

I give the property commonly known as_____

_____

to _____ or, if

_____ does not

survive me by 45 days, to _____.

6. I give my residuary estate, i.e., the rest of my property not otherwise specifically and validly disposed of by this will or in any other manner, to _____ or if _____ fails to survive me by 45 days, to

_____.

If any primary beneficiary of a shared residuary or specific gift made in this will fails to survive me by 45 days, the surviving beneficiaries of that gift shall equally divide the deceased beneficiary's share. If all primary beneficiaries of a shared residuary or specific gift fail to survive me by 45 days, that gift shall pass in equal shares to the alternate beneficiaries named to receive that gift. If the alternate beneficiaries named by this will to receive a specific gift do not survive me by 45 days, or there are no such named alternate beneficiaries, that gift shall become part of my residuary estate.

7. I nominate _____ as executor, to serve without bond. If _____ shall for any reason fail to qualify or cease to act as executor, I nominate _____ as executor, also to serve without bond. I direct that my executor take all actions legally

permissible to have the probate of my estate done as simply as possible, including filing a petition in the appropriate court for the independent administration of my estate.

[Insert executor's powers from box on page 11:55.]

8. If my _____ and I should die simultaneously, or under such circumstances
            lover/mate

as to render it difficult or impossible to determine by clear and convincing evidence who

predeceased the other, I shall be conclusively presumed to have survived my

_____ for purposes of this will.
lover/mate

I subscribe my name to this will this _____ day of _____,

19___, at _____, _____,
              city   county

_____, and do hereby declare that I sign and execute
          state

this instrument as my last will and that I sign it willingly, that I execute it as my free and

voluntary act for the purposes therein expressed, and that I am of the age of majority or

otherwise legally empowered to make a will, and under no constraint or undue influence.

_____
your signed name

On this _____ day of _____, 19___,

_____ declared to us, the undersigned, that
          your name

this instrument was _____ will and requested us to act as witnesses to it.
             his/her

_____ thereupon signed this will in our presence, all of us being present
He/She

at the same time. We now, at _____ request, in _____
                  his/her   his/her

presence, and in the presence of each other, subscribe our names as witnesses and

declare we understand this to be _____ will, and that to the best of our
                         his/her

knowledge the testator is of the age of majority, or is otherwise legally empowered to

make a will, and under no constraint or undue influence.

We declare under penalty of perjury that the foregoing is true and correct.

_____ residing at _____

_____

_____ residing at _____

_____ residing at _____

BUT IF SHE DOESN'T
SURVIVE ME .. WHO
TO LEAVE IT TO ..?

VI. Will for a Person Who Lives with a Lover/Mate and Who Has Minor Children

WILL OF _____.
your name

I, _____, a resident of
your name

_____, _____,
city   county

_____ declare that this is my will.
state

1. I revoke all wills and codicils that I have previously made.

2. My _____ name is _____, and all
lover/mate's

references in this will to my _____ are to _____.
lover/mate   him/her

[If appropriate, complete:

I was previously married to _____. That marriage was

terminated by _____.

I am the _____ of the following children, whose names and
father/mother

dates of birth are:

_____   _____
Name   Date of Birth

_____   _____
Name   Date of Birth

_____   _____
Name   Date of Birth

_____   _____
Name   Date of Birth

There are _____ living children of my deceased child _____:

_____   _____
Name of Grandchild   Date of Birth

_____   _____
Name of Grandchild   Date of Birth

_____   _____]
Name of Grandchild   Date of Birth

(repeat as needed)

3. I make the following cash gifts:

I give _____

to _____ or, if

_____ does not

survive me by 45 days, to _____.

I give _____

to _____ or, if

_____ does not

survive me by 45 days, to _____.

I give _____

to _____ or, if

_____ does not

survive me by 45 days, to _____.

I give _____

to _____ or, if

_____ does not

survive me by 45 days, to _____.

I give _____

to _____ or, if

_____ does not

survive me by 45 days, to _____.

I give _____

to _____ or, if

_____ does not

survive me by 45 days, to _____.

4. I make the following specific gifts of personal property:

I give _____

_____

to _____ or, if

_____ does not

survive me by 45 days, to _____.

I give _____

_____

to _____ or, if

_____ does not

survive me by 45 days, to _____.

I give _____

_____

to _____ or, if

_____ does not

survive me by 45 days, to _____.

I give _____

_____

to _____ or, if

_____ does not

survive me by 45 days, to _____.

I give _____

_____

to _____ or, if

_____ does not

survive me by 45 days, to _____.

I give _____

_____

to _____ or, if

_____ does not

survive me by 45 days, to _____.

5. I make the following specific gifts of real property:

I give the property commonly known as_____

_____

to _____ or, if

_____ does not

survive me by 45 days, to _____.

I give the property commonly known as_____

_____

to _____ or, if

_____ does not

survive me by 45 days, to _____.

I give the property commonly known as_____

_____

to _____ or, if

_____ does not

survive me by 45 days, to _____.

I give the property commonly known as_____

_____

to _____ or, if

_____ does not

survive me by 45 days, to _____.

6. I give my residuary estate, i.e., the rest of my property not otherwise specifically and validly disposed of by this will or in any other manner, to _____ or if _____ fails to survive me by 45 days, to

_____.

If any primary beneficiary of a shared residuary or specific gift made in this will fails to survive me by 45 days, the surviving beneficiaries of that gift shall equally divide the deceased beneficiary's share. If all primary beneficiaries of a shared residuary or specific gift fail to survive me by 45 days, that gift shall pass in equal shares to the alternate beneficiaries named to receive that gift. If the alternate beneficiaries named by this will to receive a specific gift do not survive me by 45 days, or there are no such named alternate beneficiaries, that gift shall become part of my residuary estate.

7. I nominate _____ as executor, to serve without bond. If _____ shall for any reason fail to qualify or cease to act as executor, I nominate _____ as executor, also to serve without bond. I direct that my executor take all actions legally

permissible to have the probate of my estate done as simply as possible, including filing a petition in the appropriate court for the independent administration of my estate.

[Insert executor's powers from box on page 11:55 here.]

8. If at my death any of my children are minors, and a guardian is needed, I recommend that _____ be appointed guardian of the person(s) of my minor
name

children. If _____ cannot serve as personal guardian, I
name

recommend that _____ be appointed personal guardian.
name

I appoint _____ as the property guardian of my minor
name

children. If _____ cannot serve as property guardian, I appoint
name

_____ as property guardian.
name

I direct no bond be required of any guardian.

9. All property I give in this will to any of the children listed in Section A below who are minors at my death shall be held for each of them in a separate trust, pursuant to the following trust terms, which shall apply to each trust:

A. Trust Beneficiaries and Age Limits

Each trust shall end when the following beneficiaries become 30, except as otherwise specified in this section:

Trust for   Shall end at age

_____   _____

_____   _____

_____   _____

_____   _____

_____   _____

B. Trustees

The trustee shall be _____, or, if

_____ cannot serve as trustee, the trustee shall be

_____. No bond shall be required of any trustee.

[Insert trust provisions from box on page 11:56-57 here.]

9. If my _____ and I should die simultaneously, or under such circumstances

               lover/mate

as to render it difficult or impossible to determine by clear and convincing evidence who

predeceased the other, I shall be conclusively presumed to have survived my

_____ for purposes of this will.

lover/mate

I subscribe my name to this will this _____ day of _____,

19___, at _____, _____,

                  city   county

_____, and do hereby declare that I sign and execute

            state

this instrument as my last will and that I sign it willingly, that I execute it as my free and

voluntary act for the purposes therein expressed, and that I am of the age of majority or

otherwise legally empowered to make a will, and under no constraint or undue influence.

_____

               your signed name

On this _____ day of _____, 19___,

_____ declared to us, the undersigned, that

            your name

this instrument was _____ will and requested us to act as witnesses to it.

            his/her

_____ thereupon signed this will in our presence, all of us being present

He/She

at the same time. We now, at _____ request, in _____

                      his/her   his/her

presence, and in the presence of each other, subscribe our names as witnesses and

declare we understand this to be _____ will, and that to the best of our

                                 his/her

knowledge the testator is of the age of majority, or is otherwise legally empowered to

make a will, and under no constraint or undue influence.

We declare under penalty of perjury that the foregoing is true and correct.

_____   residing at _____

_____

_____   residing at _____

_____

_____   residing at _____

_____

Executor's Powers

I hereby grant to my executor the following powers, to be exercised as he or she deems to be in the best interests of my estate:

(a) To retain property without liability for loss or depreciation resulting from such retention.

(b) To dispose of property by public or private sale, or exchange, or otherwise, and receive or administer the proceeds as a part of my estate.

(c) To vote stock, to exercise any option or privilege to convert bonds, notes, stocks or other securities belonging to my estate into other bonds, notes, stocks or other securities, and to exercise all other rights and privileges of a person owning similar property in his own right.

(d) To lease any real property that may at any time form part of my estate.

(e) To abandon, adjust, arbitrate, compromise, sue on or defend and otherwise deal with and settle claims in favor of or against my estate.

(f) To continue, maintain, operate or participate in any business which is a part of my estate, and to effect incorporation, dissolution or other change in the form of organization of the business.

(g) To pay all my debts, and all taxes that may, by reason of my death, be assessed against my estate or any portion of it, whether passing by probate or not, provided that such debts and taxes shall be first satisfied out of my residuary estate.

(h) If any person not my child who receives property under this will is a minor at the time of distribution, I direct my executor to distribute the property to the minor's custodian or guardian under the provisions of the Uniform Gifts to Minors Act, or the Uniform Transfers to Minors Act, if either is applicable.

(i) To do all other acts, which in his or her judgment may be necessary or appropriate for the proper and advantageous management, investment and distribution of my estate.

The foregoing powers, authority and discretion granted to my executor are intended to be in addition to the powers, authority and discretion vested in him or her by operation of law by virtue of his or her office, and may be exercised as often as is deemed necessary or advisable, without application to or approval by any court in any jurisdiction.

Trust Provisions

C. Beneficiary Provisions

(1) As long as a child is a beneficiary of this trust, the trustee may distribute from time to time to or for the benefit of the beneficiary as much, or all, of the net income or principal of the trust, or both, as the trustee deems necessary for the beneficiary's health, support, maintenance, and education.

Education includes, but is not limited to, college, graduate, postgraduate, and vocational studies, and reasonably related living expenses.

(2) In deciding whether to make a distribution to the beneficiary, the trustee may take into account the beneficiary's other income, resources, and sources of support.

(3) Any trust income which is not distributed to a beneficiary by the trustee shall be accumulated and added to the principal of the trust administered for that beneficiary.

D. Termination of Trust

The trust shall terminate when any of the following events occur:

(1) The beneficiary becomes the age specified in Paragraph A of this trust;

(2) The beneficiary dies before becoming the age specified in Paragraph A of this trust;

(3) The trust is exhausted through distributions allowed under these provisions.

If the trust terminates for reason (1), the remaining principal and accumulated net income of the trust shall pass to the beneficiary. If the trust terminates for reason (2), the remaining principal and accumulated net income of the trust shall pass to the residuary beneficiaries named in this will, if any, otherwise to the trust beneficiary's heirs.

E. Powers of Trustee

In addition to other powers granted the trustee in this will, the trustee shall have:

(1) All the powers generally conferred on trustees by the laws of the state having jurisdiction over this trust;

(2) In respect to property in the trust, the powers conferred by this will on the executor; and

(3) The authority to hire and pay from the trust assets the reasonable fees of investment advisors, accountants, tax advisors, agents, attorneys, and other assistants for the administration of the trust and for the management of any trust asset and for any litigation affecting the trust.

F. Trust Administrative Provisions

(1) It is my intent that this trust be administered independent of court supervision to the maximum extent possible under the laws of the state having jurisdiction over this trust.

(2) The interests of trust beneficiaries shall not be transferable by voluntary or involuntary assignment or by operation of law and shall be free from the claims of creditors and from attachment, execution, bankruptcy, or other legal process to the fullest extent permissible by law.

(3) Any trustee serving hereunder shall be entitled to reasonable compensation out of the trust assets for ordinary and extraordinary services, and for all services in connection with the complete or partial termination of any trust created by this will.

(4) The invalidity of any provision of this trust instrument shall not affect the validity of the remaining provisions.

CHAPTER 12:

Assemble the Clauses Will

A. How to Prepare Your Own Will

This chapter presents you with a series of will clauses identified by small letters "a through z." Each lettered clause covers a basic component of a will and is accompanied, where appropriate, by:

• A brief discussion of the reasons for its inclusion;

• A cross-reference to the section of the book where the particular legal issue covered in the clause is discussed in more detail; and

• An indication of whether that clause or its equivalent must be included in your will. I do this by making some clauses "mandatory" while others are "optional," to be included or not, depending on your family situation and personal desires.

For several will clauses I present two or more alternates. In this situation, it's up to you to choose the one that best meets your needs. Again, there are accompanying explanations to help you do this.

Example: Clause o is entitled "Executor(s) Clause - Mandatory." Alternative 1 provides you with a clause to appoint a single executor. Alternative 2 presents a clause for the appointment of dual executors. After referring back to Chapter 3, where you already tentatively decided on your executor(s), your job is to select the clause that best fits your needs, and write in the appropriate name or names.

To use this chapter to prepare your will, read it through at least once. Then return, and, with pencil in hand, go through it section-by-section, clause-by-clause, following these steps:

STEP1. Identify all mandatory will clauses. This is easy as they are labelled "**Mandatory**." In addition, all mandatory clauses are pre-marked with a large check mark in the box in the margin like this: ☑ If there is more than one alternative to a mandatory clause, be sure you select the one that best meets your needs;

STEP 2. Identify the optional will clauses (marked "**Optional**") you want to include in your will. Any clause which does not apply to <u>all</u> people is labelled "Optional," even if it is vital for those who do need it. For example, **clause q** provides 3 alternate choices for naming personal guardian(s) for minor children. This clause is labelled "Optional" because many readers do not have minor children. However, if you do have minor children, you definitely should complete one of the choices in **clause q**.

When you decide to use an optional clause, place a check mark in the empty box ☑ in the margin next to the selected clause. These checkmarks will be a big help when it comes time for you to type (or have typed) the final version of your will.

STEP 3. Number all the checked clauses sequentially, starting with number 1.[1] These same numbers will be typed on your final will, to identify each clause. To make this process easy, I place a circle ◯ in the margin next to every clause and each alternate. For each clause you've included in your will, simply fill in the next available number. This may seem a little complex now, but rest assured you will find it to be easy enough when it comes time to do it.

Example: The Revocation Clause which appears at the beginning of your will (after the unnumbered identification provisions) is a mandatory clause and therefore is always numbered ①. For many people, the next clause is the Marriage and Children Clause, which, if included, is given the number ②. However, if you have never been married and have no children, you will obviously want to skip this clause. In this situation, the next clause you would normally use would be the Specific Gifts of Personal Property Clause, so you'd number this clause ②. Then continue through all clauses you've included in your will, putting the next number in the circle in the margin.

STEP 4. Fill in all necessary information in the blanks in each will clause you've selected. The clauses have adequate space to do this for most situations. However, it is possible that you will require more space. If so, you will need to use an additional sheet of paper. For example, Clause "g," which deals with specific gifts of personal property, contains space for making sixteen separate gifts. If you give gifts to more than sixteen separate persons or organizations, you'll need to create more blanks. Here's how to do it:

• Put "continued on Attachment 1" at the end of the too short space;

• Either photocopy the particular blank or blanks you need more of or write the additional clauses on a piece of typing paper. Title this sheet "Attachment 1, continuation of [clause which is being continued]," (e.g., "Attachment 1, continuation of Clause 3");

• Complete the attachment by providing all the additional information needed;

• When it's time to actually assemble your draft will, attach this page, or pages, to it;

• If you need more blanks than this book provides for a second will clause, repeat this process, numbering this Attachment 2.

---

[1]The identification provisions which come at the top of your will do not carry a number.

STEP 5. When you have completed filling in all the necessary blanks and numbered the clauses you wish to include, you are ready to have your will typed. If someone else will type your will, be sure he knows exactly what's to be typed. The best way to achieve this is as follows:

• Tear out the pages containing the clauses with checked boxes. Each of these should be filled out (where appropriate) and numbered sequentially as we indicate earlier. Remember to include all attachment pages. If you prefer, you can photocopy all these pages instead of removing them from the book.

• Draw an "X" through clauses you do not wish to be included.

• Draw a line through titles of clauses, explanatory language, and printed words which appear under the blank lines of the clauses so the typist doesn't mistakenly type these words. For exam - ple, in the identification clause at the beginning of your will you should pencil in your name and then delete the words "your name" below the line:

Will of _____
your name

• Finally, adapt pronouns (he, she, they, etc.) and tenses to fit your situation. For instance, Clause g, Specific Gifts of Personal Property, provides "I give _____ to _____, or, if _____ does not survive me, to _____ " This is drafted for a gift to one person. If you make a shared gift, "does" should be changed to "do." These precautions allow you to present your typist with only and precisely what you want typed in your will. Complete typing instructions are contained in Chapter 13.

B. Making Substantive Changes in Sample Clauses

If you make substantive changes in the language of a will clause printed in this chapter, you are running a risk that:

1. You won't accomplish what you wish to, and

2. You will cause ambiguities which interfere with your will's effectiveness.

For these reasons, I urge you not to change the meaning of any of these clauses without checking the result with an attorney.

C. Prepare Your Will - Clause By Clause

Now it's time to complete the clauses for inclusion in your will.

☑ Clause a. Will Caption Clause - Mandatory

This unnumbered caption is typed at the top of your will. Use the name you commonly use for signing legal papers and other important documents. If for any reason you've used different names—e.g., you changed your name to Sara Burns but still own some property in the name of Sara Burnstein, identify yourself with both names, as "Sara Burns A/K/A/ Sara Burnstein," and sign your will that way. If there is any question about where you reside, see Chapter 2, Section A.

Will of _____
                        your name

☑ Clause b.   Personal Identification Provision Clause—Mandatory

This unnumbered provision identifies you. Use the same form of your name set out in clause a and your permanent address.

I, _____, a resident of
                        your name

_____, _____ ,
          city   county

_____ declare that this is my will.
          state

☑ Clause c. Revocation Clause—Mandatory

This clause revokes all previous wills and codicils (formal amendments to a will) which you've made. If you know the date of your most recent will (if you have one), it's helpful to both specify that date and destroy that will and all copies, but this isn't required. This is the first numbered clause of your will.

(1)   I revoke all wills and codicils I have previously made (including the will dated
_____, 19_____).

☐   **Clause d.   Marriages and Children Clause—Optional
           unless you have a current spouse, former
           spouse, children or grandchildren who are
           children of a deceased child**

If you have never been married nor had any children, skip this clause. Otherwise, place a check in the box in the margin to indicate that this clause is to be included in your will and place number (2) in the circle to indicate that this is the second clause in your will. Then fill in the blanks by listing your current spouse, if you have one, all former marriages and how they ended (e.g., by divorce, annulment, death, arsenic, etc.)., all your children, and any grandchild of yours who is the son or daughter of a child who died. As you know from Chapter 7, Section D, you must either provide in your will for each living child (and any children of a deceased child) or specifically disinherit them to be sure to avoid the "pretermitted" heir problem.

◯   I am married to _____ and all references in
this will to my spouse are to _____.
                                             him/her

I was previously married to _____. That marriage
was terminated by _____.

[repeat as needed]

I have _____ children now living, whose names and dates of birth are:
            number

_____   _____
Name   **Date of Birth**

_____   _____
Name   **Date of Birth**

_____   _____
Name   **Date of Birth**

_____   _____
Name   **Date of Birth**

_____   _____
Name   **Date of Birth**

_____   _____
Name   **Date of Birth**

_____   _____
Name   Date of Birth

[repeat as needed]

There are _____ living children of my deceased child, _____
                        number

_____:
                   name

_____   _____
Name of grandchild   Date of Birth

_____   _____
Name of grandchild   Date of Birth

_____   _____
Name of grandchild   Date of Birth

[repeat as needed]

☐ Clause e. Disinheritance Clause—Optional

If you do not plan to leave something (even $1.00, or an heirloom, or a share of your residuary estate) to each of the children you've listed above, you must specifically disinherit that child or risk a successful will challenge. To do so, check the box in the margin and number this clause with the next available number. Otherwise, leave both box and circle blank and simply skip this clause:

○   I specifically direct that _____ be

disinherited and receive nothing from my estate.

[repeat as needed]

☐ Clause f.   Specific Gifts of Cash—Optional unless you are making a cash gift in your will

If you desire to make one or more cash gifts, including money in checking, savings and money market accounts and certificates of deposits, treasury bills and notes, etc., check the box. Otherwise, proceed to Clause g.

Here you enter each cash gift you listed in Chapter 6 along with the names of the primary and alternate beneficiaries you named to receive these gifts.

◯   I make the following gifts of cash:

I give _____

to _____ or, if

_____ does not

survive me, to _____ .

I give _____

to _____ or, if

_____ does not

survive me, to _____ .

I give _____

to _____ or, if

_____ does not

survive me, to _____ .

I give _____

to _____ or, if

_____ does not

survive me, to _____ .

I give _____

to _____ or, if

_____ does not

survive me, to _____ .

I give _____

to _____ or, if

_____ does not

survive me, to _____ .

☐ Clause g.   Specific Gifts of Personal Property—Optional unless you make specific gifts of personal property in your will

Here you complete the clause necessary to make specific gifts of your personal property other than cash gifts, which you just covered. Do not use this clause for gifts of real estate, which are covered in Clause i. Assuming you wish to make specific gifts of personal property, check the box and keep reading. Otherwise leave the box blank and proceed to clause h.

You made your decisions regarding these components in Chapters 5 and 6. Now, you only need transfer the descriptions of your property set out in Chapter 5[2] and the beneficiaries (and alternate beneficiaries) you have selected to receive it set out in Chapter 6 to the appropriate lines below. Remember, you can include more than one item of property in a single gift, if you desire.

○   I make the following specific gifts of personal property:

I give _____

_____

to _____ or, if

_____ does not

survive me, to _____ .

---

[2]If you didn't use the property inventory chart in Chapter 5 because of the simplicity of your desires and/or property situation, review our guidelines for describing property provided in that chapter (Section A) prior to describing the property here.

I give _____

_____

to _____ or, if

_____ does not

survive me, to _____ .

I give _____

_____

to _____ or, if

_____ does not

survive me, to _____ .

I give _____

_____

to _____ or, if

_____ does not

survive me, to _____ .

I give _____

_____

to _____ or, if

_____ does not

survive me, to _____ .

I give _____

_____

to _____ or, if

_____ does not

survive me, to _____ .

I give _____

_____

to _____ or, if

_____ does not

survive me, to _____ .

   I give _____

_____

to _____ or, if

_____ does not

survive me, to _____ .

   I give _____

_____

to _____ or, if

_____ does not

survive me, to _____ .

   I give _____

_____

to _____ or, if

_____ does not

survive me, to _____ .

   I give _____

_____

to _____ or, if

_____ does not

survive me, to _____ .

   I give _____

_____

to _____ or, if

_____ does not

survive me, to _____ .

I give _____

_____

to _____ or, if

_____ does not

survive me, to _____ .

I give _____

_____

to _____ or, if

_____ does not

survive me, to _____ .

I give _____

_____

to _____ or, if

_____ does not

survive me, to _____ .

I give _____

_____

to _____ or, if

_____ does not

survive me, to _____ .

☐ Clause h. Debts Forgiven—Optional unless you forgive debts

You can use your will to forgive debts. If you wish to, return to Chapter 6 where you described the debts to be forgiven and enter the information below. If you do, check the box. Otherwise leave it blank.

Reminder: If you are married and wish to use your will to forgive a debt, be sure you have full power to do so. This may not be the case if the money is owed to both you and your spouse. (See Chapter 4.)

◯   I forgive my interest in the following debts, including all interest accrued as of the date of my death:

Person(s) or organizations	Date of loan	Approximate amount of debt plus interest at date of will signing
_____	_____	_____
_____	_____	_____
_____	_____	_____
_____	_____	_____

☐ ### Clause i.   Gifts of Real Estate—Optional unless you want to leave real property in your will

Assuming you own some real estate, check the box in the margin. Then complete the real estate clauses by transferring the property description information from the chart in Chapter 5[3] and your choice of a beneficiary (and alternate beneficiary) from Chapter 6 to the clause below. Each parcel of real estate you own, including any condominiums or co-ops, should be listed in your will separately.

▲ Using the Will Book, all real estate must be left outright to some person(s) and/or organization(s). As previously discussed, if you want to leave a "life estate" interest in any of your real estate, see a lawyer.

Now, complete the clauses.

○ I make the following gifts of real estate:

I give the property commonly known as _____

_____

to _____ , or, if

_____ does not survive

me, to _____ .

I give the property commonly known as _____

_____

to _____ , or, if

_____
[3]See the previous footnote.

_____ does not survive

me, to _____ .

I give the property commonly known as _____

_____

to _____ , or, if

_____ does not survive

me, to _____ .

I give the property commonly known as _____

_____

to _____ , or, if

_____ does not survive

me, to _____ .

I give the property commonly known as _____

_____

to _____ , or, if

_____ does not survive

me, to _____ .

I give the property commonly known as _____

_____

to _____ , or, if

_____ does not survive

me, to _____ .

Clause j. Encumbrances on Real Property—Optional

When you give a gift of real property, the recipient is responsible for all encumbrances unless you specify differently in your will. Occasionally, however, a person wants to leave a piece of real estate free of all encumbrances because the recipient cannot pay them or would be hard pressed to do so. If you want to vary the general rule and relieve the beneficiary of this obligation, you must put a clause in your will saying so. Of course, you must be sure there's enough money elsewhere in your estate to pay the encumbrances. Usually, if a person wishes to relieve a beneficiary of real property of the obligation to pay mortgage debts, tax liens, etc., they indicate that these should be paid from your residuary estate.

Note that the clause below applies to one specific gift of real estate only. If you want to give more than one gift of real estate free of encumbrances, repeat this clause for each such gift. Two additional clauses are provided for this purpose. Also, this clause should not be used for any real property that you plan to leave as part of your residuary estate. If you use this clause, remember to check the box in the margin.

I direct that the gift of real estate, _____

                                                                          address

_____ given to _____,

                                                         beneficiary

be made free of all encumbrances on that property at my death, including but not limited

to any mortgages, deeds of trust, real property taxes and assessments, and estate and

inheritance taxes, and that such encumbrances shall be paid by my executor from

_____.

                                                         source

I direct that the gift of real estate, _____
address

_____ given to _____,
beneficiary

be made free of all encumbrances on that property at my death, including but not limited to any mortgages, deeds of trust, real property taxes and assessments, and estate and inheritance taxes, and that such encumbrances shall be paid by my executor from

_____.
source

I direct that the gift of real estate, _____
address

_____ given to _____,
beneficiary

be made free of all encumbrances on that property at my death, including but not limited to any mortgages, deeds of trust, real property taxes and assessments, and estate and inheritance taxes, and that such encumbrances shall be paid by my executor from

_____.
source

☑ Clause k. Residuary Clause—Mandatory

As previously discussed, the "residue" of your estate is exactly what it sounds like—all that remains after all cash gifts, specific gifts of personal property and gifts of real estate have been distributed. Whether your residue consists of a significant amount of property obviously depends on whether you have given most of your property away via specific gifts. Sometimes people make only a few specific gifts, and leave the bulk of their property in their residue. Also, if you get a windfall shortly before you die—win a lottery, receive a surprise inheritance—and do not make specific provision to leave it to a named beneficiary, it becomes part of your residue.

As you know from reading Chapter 6, the person who gets your residue is called "the residuary beneficiary." In addition to providing for your primary and alternate residuary beneficiaries, the residuary clause set out below also provides that:

• Alternate beneficiaries of shared gifts (both specific and residuary) only take the gift if all the primary beneficiaries fail to survive you by the time period specified in your will; and

• Specific gifts shall pass into your residuary estate in the event all the primary and alternate beneficiaries you name to receive the gift fail to survive you by the time period specified in your will. You will have the opportunity to choose a survivorship period in clause l.

Reminder: You should always name at least one alternate beneficiary for your residue. If you decide to leave your residue to more than one primary beneficiary, you may also name alternate beneficiaries as well. However, as with the specific gifts, if one of the primary beneficiaries fails to survive you by the period specified in the will, the surviving beneficiaries take that beneficiary's share. Only if all the primary residuary beneficiaries fail to survive you by your survivorship period will your named alternate receive the residue. Thus, if you name your three children as residuary beneficiaries and a cousin as the alternate beneficiary, and one of your children predeceases you, the two surviving children will inherit all of your residuary estate and your cousin will inherit nothing.

You have already named the beneficiary, or beneficiaries, for your residue, and the alternate(s), in the chart in Chapter 6. Turn back to that chart now and transfer that information to the clause below.

○   I give my residuary estate, i.e., the rest of my property not otherwise specifically and validly disposed of by this will or in any other manner, to _____

_____, or, if _____

fails to survive me, to _____.

If any primary beneficiary of a shared residuary gift or shared specific gift made in this will fails to survive me by the period specified in this will, the surviving beneficiaries of that gift shall equally divide the deceased beneficiary's share. If all primary beneficiaries of a shared residuary gift or shared specific gift fail to survive me by the period specified in the will, that gift shall pass in equal shares to the alternate beneficiaries named to receive that gift. If the alternate beneficiaries named by this will to receive a specific gift do not survive me by the period specified in this will, or there are no such named alternate beneficiaries, that gift shall become part of my residuary estate.

☑

Clause I. Survivorship Period Clause—Mandatory

As discussed in Chapter 6, a "survivorship period" clause requires a beneficiary to survive you by a specified time. If the named beneficiary does not survive you by this time period, the property goes to whoever you've specified as your alternate beneficiary (or to the surviving beneficiaries if you've named more than one), or if they fail to survive you, the gift then becomes part of the residue.

As discussed in Chapter 6, survivorship clauses can be valuable to prevent the possibility of your property from being tangled up in two probates—yours and that of the beneficiary who is to receive that property should that person die soon after you do. I recommend a 45 day survivorship period, at a minimum, and 180 days at a maximum. If you desire a longer period see an attorney. If you don't desire any period at all, simply put zero in the indicated blank.

○   All primary, alternate and residuary beneficiaries named in this will are required to survive me by _____ days as a condition of receiving any gift under the terms of this will.

☐ **Clause m. Abatement Clauses—Optional**

These two optional clauses specify what happens if at your death you do not own property of sufficient value to cover all your cash gifts after your debts and taxes are paid. This issue is dis-cussed in Chapter 6. If you don't include one of these clauses, the laws of your state govern this issue. If you do wish to include one of these clauses, remember to check the box and number the clause you choose (only choose one).

Alternative 1 - Abatement First from Residue

○   If my estate is not sufficient to pay in full all cash gifts I have made in this will, my executor shall first sell the personal property, and then the real property, in my residuary estate, in the amount necessary to pay these gifts.

Alternative 2 - Abatement Pro-Rata from Cash Gifts First

○   If my estate is not sufficient to pay all cash gifts I have made in this will in full, the executor shall make an appropriate pro-rata reduction of each cash gift.

☐ **Clause n.   Payment of Death Taxes and Debts Clause— Optional**

Your estate is obligated to pay your debts and taxes, including all death taxes. These may be minimal, or even non-existent, and thus not worth bothering about in your will. Routine debts for charge accounts and personal services (e.g., the gardener or housekeeper) are normally paid by a surviving spouse or family member out of liquid assets left in a checking or savings account and do not need to be separately provided for. However, if your debts are substantial, or if your estate is large enough (over $600,000 in 1987 and thereafter) to be subject to federal estate taxes (see Chapter 8), you may want to specify that certain assets be used to pay your debts and taxes. If you don't, the cost of paying your debts and taxes may be paid from the residue or be pro-rated against all property in your estate, depending on the laws of your state.

You may also want to give some gifts of personal property free of all liability for debts and taxes (encumbrances on real estate aren't included here, as they were covered in Clause j). Similarly, you may want your debts and taxes paid from certain assets, such as defined bank accounts.

To achieve these desires, check the box and use or adapt one of the following clauses:

Alternative 1: Residue Pays for Debts and Death Taxes

○   Except as otherwise specifically provided in this will, I direct that my executor shall pay all my debts and inheritance, estate or other death taxes out of the residue of my estate.

Alternative 2: Debts and Taxes Paid for Out of Specific Assets

○   Except as otherwise specifically provided in this will, I direct that my executor shall pay all my debts and all inheritance, estate or other death taxes assessed against my estate from _____
identify asset

Note: In this clause do not specify any item of real property which you are giving free of encumbrances under Clause j; you have already left this property free of encumbrances.

Alternative 3: Exempting Specific Gifts from Liability for Debts and Taxes

[Repeat as often as needed]

○   I direct that the gift _____
identify gift

given to_____
name beneficiaries

be given free of any liability for debts or inheritance, estate or other death taxes assessed against my estate.

 ## Clause o. Executor(s) Clause—Mandatory

You already decided upon your executor(s) and successor executor(s) in Chapter 3. Now select an executor clause from the two alternatives below and enter your choices from Chapter 3.

Alternative 1: Sole Executor Clause

○   I nominate _____ as executor , to serve without bond. If _____ shall for any reason fail to qualify or cease to act as executor, I nominate _____ _____, also to serve without bond.

Alternative 2: Dual Executors

○ I nominate _____ and
_____ to serve as executors
without bond. If either of these persons fails to survive me, or is otherwise unavailable to
serve, the remaining surviving executor shall function as a sole executor also without
bond. If both of these persons fail to survive me, or are otherwise unavailable to serve, I
nominate _____
_____ to serve as executor
without bond.

☑ ### Clause p. Executor's Powers Clause—Mandatory

In the clause below, you'll find the standard Nolo Will clause for executor's powers. This clause must be included in all wills drafted in this chapter. It gives your executor a good deal of flexibility, which is generally desirable. ▲ Occasionally people wish to limit the power of their executor or give her special instructions or duties. If you find yourself in this situation, see a lawyer.

○ #### Executor's Powers
Except as otherwise provided in my will, I hereby grant to my executor the following powers, to be exercised as he or she deems to be in the best interests of my estate:
(a) To retain property without liability for loss or depreciation resulting from such retention.
(b) To dispose of property by public or private sale, or exchange, or otherwise, and receive or administer the proceeds as a part of my estate.
(c) To vote stock, to exercise any option or privilege to convert bonds, notes, stocks or other securities belonging to my estate into other bonds, notes, stocks or other securities, and to exercise all other rights and privileges of a person owning similar property in his own right.
(d) To lease any real property that may at any time form part of my estate.
(e) To abandon, adjust, arbitrate, compromise, sue on or defend and otherwise deal with and settle claims in favor of or against my estate.
(f) To continue, maintain, operate or participate in any business which is a part of my estate, and to effect incorporation, dissolution or other change in the form of organization of the business.
(g) To pay all my debts, and all taxes that may, by reason of my death, be assessed against my estate or any portion of it, whether passing by probate or not.
(h) To do all other acts, which in his or her judgment may be necessary or appropriate for the proper and advantageous management, investment and distribution of my estate.

The foregoing powers, authority and discretion granted to my executor are intended to be in addition to the powers, authority and discretion vested in him or her by operation of law by virtue of his or her office, and may be exercised as often as is deemed necessary or advisable, without application to or approval by any court in any jurisdiction.

Clause q. Personal Guardian of Minor Children Clause—Optional

Reminder: As I said in Section A, clause 2, if you have minor children, this clause is mandatory for you.

You've already named your preferences for the primary and successor personal guardians of your minor children (if there is no living person entitled to legal custody who is available to assume it). See Chapter 7. Now is the time to put these choices in your will.

Alternative 1: Guardian Appointment Clause for Use by Member of a Couple

If at my death any of my children are minors and a guardian is needed, I recommend that _____be appointed
                                                    name
guardian of the person(s) of my minor children. If _____
                                                                        name
_____cannot serve as guardian, I recommend

that _____be appointed
                                            name
personal guardian. I direct that no bond be required of any personal guardians.

Optional Addition: Statement of Reasons For Designating of Guardian

I believe it is in the best interests of my children for _____

_____ to be their guardian because

_____

_____

_____

_____.

Alternative 2:   Guardian Appointment Clause for a Parent With Other Parent Living but Not Desired as Child(ren)'s Guardian[4]

If at my death any of my children are minors and a guardian is needed, I recommend that _____ be appointed guardian of
                                                    name
the person(s) of my minor children. If_____
                                                    name
cannot serve as guardian, I recommend that _____
                                                    name
_____be appointed personal guardian. I direct that no bond be

required of any personal guardian.

I believe it is in the best interests of my children for _____
                                                    name
_____to be their guardian, rather than _____

_____because _____
              natural parent's name

_____

_____

_____

Alternative 3: Different Guardians for Different Children

If at my death any of my children are minors and a guardian is needed:

I recommend that_____be appointed
                                        name
guardian of my child(ren) _____, _____,

_____. If _____
                                                    name
cannot serve as guardian, I recommend that _____
                                                    name

---

[4]Reread the discussion in Chapter 7 before using this alternative. The other natural parent usually gets custody (unless he or she is unfit or unavailable), regardless of your desires.

be appointed personal guardian for these children.

I recommend that_____be appointed
name

guardian of my child(ren) _____, _____,

_____. If _____
name

cannot serve as guardian, I recommend that _____
name

be appointed personal guardian for these children.

I direct that no bond be required of any personal guardian.

I believe these people are the best guardians for the respective children because ___

_____

_____

_____

_____

_____

Clause r. Guardian for Property of Your Children—Optional

As previously discussed, you should always have a guardian to manage the property owned by your minor children. You chose that guardian in Chapter 7, Section C. Here you record that choice which may well be the same person you named as a personal guardian.

Alternative 1: Property Guardian Appointment

If at my death any of my children are minors, I appoint _____
name

_____property guardian of my minor children. If_____
name

_____cannot serve as property guardian, I

appoint_____
name

as property guardian.

I direct that no bond be required of any property guardian.

Alternative 2: Different Property Guardians for Different Children Clause

If at my death any of my children are minors, I appoint _____
name
to be property guardian for my children _____ ,

_____ , and _____ . If

_____ cannot serve as guardian, I appoint
name
_____ as property guardian for these children.
name

I direct that no bond be required of any property guardian.

I believe these are the best property guardians for my children because: _____

_____

_____

_____

_____

_____

_____

If at my death any of my children are minors, I appoint _____
name
to be property guardian for my children _____ ,

_____ , and _____ . If

_____ cannot serve as guardian, I appoint
name
_____ as property guardian for these children.
name

I direct that no bond be required of any property guardian.

I believe these are the best property guardians for my children because: _____

_____

_____

_____

_____

_____

Clause s. Trusts for Property You Leave to Your Minor Children—Optional

You may want to establish a trust if you leave substantial amounts of property to one or more of your minor children (or if you leave valuable property to your spouse and name a minor child or children as your alternate or residuary beneficiary), as discussed in Chapter 7, Section C. This trust works equally well whether you're married, single, or divorced. However, if you are married and you choose to leave most of your property to your spouse, and only to your minor children if you both die in a simultaneous death, you obviously want to choose a trustee other than your spouse.

Each trust provides that all money left to the minor children indicated in Section A of the trust is turned over to them outright at age 30, unless you specify different ages.

Trust for Property Left to Your Minor Children Clause

All property I give in this will to any of the children listed in section A below who are minors at my death shall be held for each of them in a separate trust, pursuant to the following trust terms, which shall apply to each trust:

A. Age Limit

Each trust shall end when the following beneficiaries become 30, except as otherwise specified:

Trust for   Shall end at age

_____   _____

_____   _____

_____   _____

_____   _____

_____   _____

_____   _____

B. Trustees

The trustee shall be _____, or, if

_____ cannot serve as trustee, the

trustee shall be _____. No bond shall be

required of any trustee.

C. Beneficiary Provisions

(1) As long as a child is a beneficiary of this trust, the trustee may distribute from time to time to or for the benefit of the beneficiary as much, or all, of the net income or principal of the trust, or both, as the trustee deems necessary for the beneficiary's health, support, maintenance, and education.

"Education" includes, but is not limited to, college, graduate, postgraduate, and vocational studies, and reasonably related living expenses.

(2) In deciding whether to make a distribution to the beneficiary, the trustee may take into account the beneficiary's other income, resources, and sources of support.

(3) Any trust income which is not distributed to a beneficiary by the trustee shall be accumulated and added to the principal of the trust administered for that beneficiary.

D. Termination of Trust

The trust shall terminate when any of the following events occur:

(1) The beneficiary becomes the age specified in Paragraph A of this trust;

(2) The beneficiary dies before becoming the age specified in Paragraph A of this trust;

(3) The trust is exhausted through distributions allowed under these provisions.

If the trust terminates for reason (1), the remaining principal and accumulated net income of the trust shall pass to the beneficiary. If the trust terminates for reason (2), the remaining principal and accumulated net income of the trust shall pass to the residuary beneficiaries named in this will, if any, otherwise to the trust beneficiary's heirs.

E. Powers of Trustee

In addition to other powers granted the trustee in this will, the trustee shall have:

(1) All the powers generally conferred on trustees by the laws of the state having jurisdiction over this trust;

(2) In respect to property in the trust, the powers conferred by this will on the executor; and

(3) The authority to hire and pay from the trust assets the reasonable fees of investment advisors, accountants, tax advisors, agents, attorneys, and other assistants for the administration of the trust and for the management of any trust asset and for any litigation affecting the trust.

F. Trust Administrative Provisions

(1) It is my intent that this trust be administered independent of court supervision to the maximum extent possible under the laws of the state having jurisdiction over this trust.

(2) The interests of trust beneficiaries shall not be transferable by voluntary or involuntary assignment or by operation of law and shall be free from the claims of creditors and from attachment, execution, bankruptcy, or other legal process to the fullest extent permissible by law.

(3) Any trustee serving hereunder shall be entitled to reasonable compensation out of the trust assets for ordinary and extraordinary services, and for all services in connection with the complete or partial termination of any trust created by this will.

(4) The invalidity of any provision of this trust instrument shall not affect the validity of the remaining provisions.

Clause t.   Gifts to Minors Other than Your Own Children—Optional

As discussed in Chapter 7, Section F, the simplest, best way to make gifts to other minors is through the Uniform Gifts to Minors Act (or the Uniform Transfers to Minors Act). One or the other of these very similar provisions has been adopted by all states. You only need use this clause if any of your beneficiaries (including alternate or residuary beneficiaries), other than your own children, is a minor. If you do use the clause, check the box and number the clause accordingly.

Gifts to Minors Other than Your Own Children Clause

For each beneficiary of my will, aside from my children, who is a minor at the time of distribution of gifts made to him or her, I direct my executor to distribute the property given to each such minor to that minor's parent(s) with legal custody, or, if there is (are) none, to the minor's legal guardian, as custodian under the provisions of the Uniform Gifts to Minors Act or the Uniform Transfers to Minors Act. I direct that the parents or guardian, as custodian, release such property to the minor beneficiary when he or she reaches the age of majority.

Clause u. No Contest Clause—Optional

A no contest clause is designed to discourage will contests by disinheriting anyone who unsuccessfully challenges your will. (Obviously, a successful challenge to a will sets it aside, including a no contest provision.) The gift that was to go to the contesting beneficiary goes to the alternate beneficiary or, if no alternate was named, to the residuary beneficiary. If you believe there's any likelihood someone may challenge your will, or if you're just cautious, you can include a no contest clause in your will (Remember to check the box). Generally, courts enforce such a clause.

No Contest Clause

If any beneficiary under this will in any manner, directly or indirectly, contests or attacks this will or any of its provisions, any property, share or interest in my estate given to the contesting beneficiary under this will is revoked and shall be disposed of in the same manner provided herein as if that contesting beneficiary had predeceased me without issue.

Clause v. Simultaneous Death—Optional

People often wonder and worry about what happens if they die at the same time as their spouse (or mate or lover). Who is a primary beneficiary under their will? Who gets what? As discussed in Chapter 6, Section J, survivorship clauses usually provide an orderly method for determining which heirs inherit a spouse's property when it is impossible to tell which spouse died first. Under the will you are drafting in this chapter, assuming you chose a survivorship period under clause l, all property you left to your spouse (or mate or lover) will pass to the alternates in the event of a simultaneous death. Only if there is no survivorship period, or some property is not successfully disposed of under the will, is this clause likely to come into operation. However, if you wish to include this clause in your will (it can't hurt), complete the following:

Simultaneous Death

If my _____ and I should die simultaneously,
wife/husband/mate

or under such circumstances as to render it difficult or impossible to determine by clear

and convincing evidence who predeceased the other, I shall be conclusively presumed

to have survived my _____ for purposes of this will.
wife/husband/mate

Clause w. Pets Clause—Optional

You can provide for your pets in your will.[5] The simplest way is by leaving a sum of money (and whatever directions are appropriate) to a friend (who has agreed to take on the responsibility) to provide that care. You can also provide for your pet in a more elaborate legal form, by creating a trust for it. ▲ To do that, see a lawyer.

I want my pet _____ to be well cared for, and direct that:

_____
insert your instructions

_____.

_____.

---

[5]In many areas of the country, you cannot legally direct that your healthy pet be destroyed. For example, a will provision requiring a woman's dog to be killed after her death was held unenforceable by a San Francisco court.

To achieve proper care for my pet, I leave the sum of $_____ to

_____

name

_____

address

Clause x. Body Parts Donation Clause—Optional

You may want your body to be available for medical research and/or organ transplant purposes. If so, include one or both of these alternate clauses. In many states, such as California, this clause meets all legal requirements. Because it often takes some time to locate and read a will, you also need to be sure you've arranged for the legal authorization necessary in your state, and immediate implementation of organ donation upon death.

Alternative 1: Donation of Body to Medical Institution Clause

I declare that I want to donate my body to any medical institution which will accept it, for research purposes, and I direct my executor to take all steps necessary to carry out such donations of my body.

Alternative 2: Donation of Body Parts for Organ Transplants Clause

I declare that, pursuant to the Uniform Anatomical Gift Act, I want to donate any and all of my body parts, organs, etc., to any medical facility or institution which will accept them, and I direct my executor to take all steps necessary to carry out such donation of my body parts, organs, etc.

Clause y. Burial Instructions Clause—Optional

You can include a clause regarding disposition of your body in your will. In many states, such a clause is legally binding. However, you shouldn't rely only on your will to establish a plan to dispose of your remains. Why? Because wills are often not located and read immediately after death. It is accordingly wise to leave specific instructions to those who will take responsibility for your funeral arrangements. But because putting your burial/body disposition instructions in your will gives them increased validity if someone challenges them, it is a good idea to also do this.

Note: If you want to assure that your plans are carried out, make sure your executor knows about them and has a copy of your will to back him up, should your plans be disputed after you die. It is also wise to both arrange and pay for funeral, burial or cremation details in advance.

Alternative 1: Burial/Funeral Arrangement Clause

I have made and paid for funeral arrangements with _____

_____and for burial at _____

_____, and I direct my executor to take all steps necessary to carry out such arrangements.

Alternative 2: Cremation Clause

○   I have made arrangements and paid for the cremation of my remains with _____ _____ and I direct my executor to take all steps necessary to carry out such arrangements.

☑ **Clause z. Signature and Witnessing Clause—Mandatory**

This is the final clause of your will. It is not actually numbered in your will.

I subscribe my name to this will this _____ day of _____, 19_____, at_____,
city

_____, _____
county   state

and do hereby declare that I sign and execute this instrument as my last will and that I sign it willingly, and that I execute it as my free and voluntary act for the purposes therein expressed, and that I am of the age of majority or otherwise legally empowered to make a will, and under no constraint or undue influence.

_____
your signed name

On this _____ day of _____, 19_____,
_____declared to us, the undersigned, that this
your name
instrument was _____will and requested us to act as witnesses to it.
his/her
_____ thereupon signed this will in our presence, all of us being present
He/She
at the same time. We now, at_____ request, in _____
his/her   his/her
presence, and in the presence of each other, subscribe our names as witnesses and declare we understand this to be _____will, and that to the best of our
his/her
knowledge the testator is of the age of majority, or is otherwise legally empowered to make a will, and under no constraint or undue influence.

We declare under penalty of perjury that the foregoing is true and correct.

_____ residing at

_____

_____ residing at

_____

_____ residing at

_____

D. Checklist

By now you should have:

• reviewed each clause in this chapter;

• where a mandatory clause provides alternatives, selected one of them;

• checked the boxes for each optional clause you wish to include and selected an alternative where appropriate; and

• sequentially numbered the clauses where circles are provided;

Now it's time to follow the instructions in Section A of this chapter to, cross out instructional language, make such technical changes as are obviously appropriate, etc.

E. Next Steps

You have now prepared a working draft of your will ready for final typing, signing, and witnessing. For instructions on how to accomplish these tasks (and, if you wish, make your will "self proving"), proceed to Chapter 13.

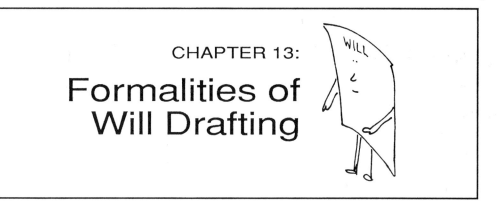

CHAPTER 13:

Formalities of Will Drafting

Let's focus now on the formal requirements necessary to make your will legal. Fortunately, they are easy. All you need to do is make sure your will is neatly typed and then you sign it in front of three witnesses and have them sign it as well. Let's examine both of these formalities in detail.

Important: If your will does not comply with the technical requirements—say it was typed but not witnessed—the will cannot be validated by the probate court, and your property will pass as if no will existed. It's not hard to prepare a will correctly. But it is essential to check and doublecheck to be sure you do.

A. Type Your Will

The final will you prepare from the Will Book must be completely typewritten. The typing machine can be an old portable or a sophisticated computer printer, as long as it prints clearly. This means you must take the draft will you have prepared (whether a basic form will from Chapter 11 or one you've assembled from Chapter 12) and either type the entire document yourself or have it typed. It is not advisable and may not be legal to use a typewriter to fill in the blanks of a will form in this book and sign and witness that document as your will.

If you cannot type yourself, you obviously must arrange to have the will typed by someone else. Typing services are available through the yellow pages. Most charge about $25 per hour, which means that unless your will is very long, you shouldn't pay more than $50 to have it typed.

Your will should be typed on regular 8-1/2" x 11" white bond typing paper. It's preferable not to use erasable typing paper. Paper with a high rag content looks nicer, but cheap paper is just as legal. I recommend double spacing, although single spacing is permissible. Spacing should be uniform throughout the will. Normal side and top margins are acceptable (one inch on all sides is recommended), and no abnormal gaps should be present on any page.

Once your will is complete you may want to staple it to a heavy sheet of backing paper that identifies it as your will. You can purchase a backing sheet from a stationery store or from Nolo as part of a Nolo Will Paper Kit, which also includes rag content paper and a storage envelope (see back of this book for details).

Typing mistakes can be machine corrected, but there can be no handwritten corrections or cross-outs. If you X out, or type over, a mistake, you may invalidate your will. Allowable machine corrections include use of self-correcting typewriters, and careful use of white-out, or correcting tape, and then retyping. However, do not do this extensively. If you make more than a few minor changes, retype your will.

Common Sense Note: Your primary mission when you type your will is to avoid any remote suspicion that you or anyone else changed your will after you engaged in the formal signing and witnessing ceremony. Accordingly, if a mistake is made on a sensitive item, say a beneficiary's name, you should retype the whole page rather than using white-out or something similar. You do not want to create the possibility that either an heir or the probate court will ask how the change was made.

B. Staple Your Will

Once your will is typed, simply staple it together in the upper lefthand corner with one or two heavy duty staples.

C. Requirements for Signing and Witnessing Your Will

Now let's briefly review the proper procedures for signing and witnessing your will.

1. Signing Your Will

In legalese, signing your will is called the "execution" or the "acknowledgment" of the will. This means that you must date the will and sign it at the end in the presence of witnesses. The date is the day, month and year you sign the will. Your signature should be made in ink and should be in exactly the same form of your name you used in your will. In other words, if you commonly use a middle initial (or full middle name) and type your name that way in your will, sign it the same way. For example, if you start your will with the name of Elissa T. James, sign your will the same way, not in another form, such as "E. T. James," or "Elissa Thelma James."

You are not legally required to sign or initial every page of your will. However, if you are the cautious type, feel free to do so. The purpose of initialing every page of a will is to protect against the remote chance that some evil-doer will remove a page from your will and substitute a fraudulent page after you die. If you want to gain whatever added protection initializing or signing each page provides, do so on the lower right margin.

2. Witnessing Your Will

Under the law of every state, your signature on a formal typed will must be witnessed to be valid. This means that your witnesses must watch you sign the will and then sign their names, below your signature. Here's is a step-by-step breakdown of how to accomplish this:

a. Use Three Witnesses

While state laws vary as to witnesses' requirements, having three people witness a will meets the legal requirements of all states. Even if the law of your state only requires two witnesses, three is better because it provides one more person to establish that your signature is valid should this become necessary during probate.

b. Who to Select as Your Witnesses

Here are the guidelines you should follow in selecting your witnesses. Each witness must be:

• A legally competent adult;

• Not a beneficiary of your will. This is important—if you leave property to a witness he may be disqualified from inheriting;

• If possible, a person likely to be easy to locate when you die. This usually means choosing people who know you and who live in your area, don't move around a lot and are younger than you are. Using witnesses who live far away does not invalidate your will, but it can make it more difficult for your executor to produce the witnesses in court should this be required as part of pro - bating your estate. Many states have substantially eliminated the requirement that a witness actu - ally appear in court and testify in the probate proceeding. Instead, a written affidavit from the witnesses is deemed sufficient. However, a minority of states still require witness testimony in court. Also in rare circumstances, such as a will contest, the court testimony and character of your witnesses could be crucial. It's also a sensible idea to keep track of the location of your witnesses, and record their current addresses so your executor can readily locate them.

c. The Witnesses Must Witness You Signing Your Will

When you are ready to sign your will, assemble all your witnesses. There is absolutely no requirement that the witnesses read your will or that you read it to them. However, they must all realize that you intend the document to be your will. Traditionally, there's a ritual dialogue engaged in which sounds like something from a Gilbert and Sullivan operetta, but it does satisfy the technicalities of the law:

You say: "This is my will."

Your witnesses say (in unison or individually): "He says it is his will."

Then you sign your will, and immediately after that the witnesses sign it in ink with their normal handwritten signatures. The witnesses' addresses are not legally required, but it's a good idea to list them for identification and possibly to help locate them after your death.

D. Using a Notary Public

In no state does a will legally have to be notarized.[1] However, in most states you can poten - tially simplify the probate process if you and your witnesses sign a simple affidavit in front of a notary public declaring that the document is your will and that it was properly executed. This affidavit is then attached to your will. This whole process is called creating a "self-proving" will. It's important to reiterate that self-proving your will does not affect its validity.

The reason for self-proving your will is to eliminate the requirement that a witness appear at the probate proceeding after your death. This of course is particularly useful if your witnesses can't be found. However, there's now a strong national trend among the states to allow witnesses to a will to declare in an affidavit prepared after your death that they in fact witnessed the will (as opposed to actually appearing and testifying to this in court), accordingly, including a self-proving affidavit with your will may not be the only way you can free your witnesses from the necessity of appearing in court.

If you desire to make your will self-proving, take the following steps:

1. Do not use a self-proving affidavit if you are a resident of California, Maryland, Michigan, Ohio, Vermont, Wisconsin, or Washington D.C. These states do not recognize the self-proving option. ▲ Also, if you are in New Hampshire, see a lawyer for the precise language needed for your state's self-proving will.

2. Sign your will, and have it witnessed, as described in Chapter 11.

3. Either have a notary present at the will signing, or find a notary at a later time. Either way, you and your three witnesses must personally appear before the notary and be prepared to identify yourselves.

4. Tell the notary that you want to make your will self-proving and ask whether he or she has a form for doing that. If so, use that form and follow the notary's instructions.

5. If the notary doesn't have the form, select the correct form provided here, tear it out, and prepare it following the instructions.

People in the following states should use Form 1:

Alabama, Alaska, Arizona, Arkansas, Colorado, Connecticut, Hawaii, Idaho, Illinois, Indiana, Maine, Minnesota, Mississippi, Montana, Nebraska, Nevada, New Mexico, New York, North Dakota, Oregon, South Carolina, South Dakota, Tennessee, Utah, Washington, and West Virginia.

People in the following states should use Form 2:

Delaware, Florida, Georgia, Iowa, Kansas, Kentucky, Massachusetts, Missouri, New Jersey, North Carolina, Oklahoma, Pennsylvania, Rhode Island, Texas, Virginia, and Wyoming.

6. Put your name and your witnesses' names in the spaces indicated in the affidavit, and give it to the notary. He or she will have you and your witnesses swear to the truth of the statement in the affidavit (which basically are the same statements you used when the will itself was being signed and witnessed) and will then date and sign the affidavit and put his or her notary seal on it.

---

[1] Except Louisiana. Louisiana law is substantially different from that in the other 49 states. This book does not apply to and should not be used in Louisiana.

7. Staple the affidavit to your will. If you ever make a new will or codicil, you should also redo your affidavit.

Reminder: Both you and your witnesses must sign your will in addition to signing this affidavit. The affidavit and will are two separate documents.

Form 1

Affidavit

STATE OF _____

COUNTY OF _____

I, the undersigned, an officer authorized to administer oaths, certify that

_____, the testator, and _____

_____, and _____

the witnesses, whose names are signed to the attached or foregoing instrument and whose signature appears below, having appeared together before me and having been first duly sworn, each then declared to me that: 1) the attached or foregoing instrument is the last will of the testator; 2) the testator willingly and voluntarily declared, signed and executed the will in the presence of the witnesses; 3) the witnesses signed the will upon request by the testator, in the presence and hearing of the testator, and in the presence of each other; 4) to the best knowledge of each witness the testator was, at that time of the signing, of the age of majority (or otherwise legally competent to make a will), of sound mind, and under no constraint or undue influence; and 5) each witness was and is competent and of the proper age to witness a will.

Testator: _____

Witness: _____

Witness: _____

Witness: _____

Subscribed, sworn and acknowledged before me by _____

the testator, and by _____, _____, and

_____ witnesses, this _____ day of _____, 19____.

SIGNED: _____

_____
OFFICIAL CAPACITY OF OFFICER

Form 2

AFFIDAVIT

We, _____, _____,
_____, and _____
the testator and the witnesses, respectively, whose names are signed to the attached or
foregoing instrument in those capacities, personally appearing before the undersigned
authority and being first duly sworn, declare to the undersigned authority under penalty
of perjury that: 1) the testator declared, signed and executed the instrument as his/her
last will; 2) he/she signed it willingly or directed another to sign for him/her; 3) he/she
executed it as his/her free and voluntary act for the purposes therein expressed; and 4)
each of the witnesses, at the request of the testator, in his/her hearing and presence,
and in the presence of each other, signed the will as witness and that to the best of
his/her knowledge the testator was at that time of full legal age, of sound mind and under
no constraint or undue influence.

Testator: _____

Witness: _____

Witness: _____

Witness: _____

Subscribed, sworn and acknowledged before me by _____
the testator, and by _____ , _____ , and
_____ witnesses, this _____ day of _____, 19____.

SIGNED: _____

_____
OFFICIAL CAPACITY OF OFFICER

CHAPTER 14:
After Your Will Is Completed

Once your will is typed, double-checked, stapled together, signed and witnessed (in front of a notary if you want it to be self-proving), you are done. Congratulations! You've completed an important job. For some, a party celebrating the completion oif the will can be fun. Why not gather those you love, break out some good brandy (or soda, if you prefer) reveal as much (or as little) of your will as you want to, and enjoy? Your next question is normally where to keep your will, who to give copies to, and, perhaps eventually, how to legally update it.

A. Copying and Storing Your Will

After you've prepared a valid will, what do you do with it? Your main consideration should be that upon your death the right people—at a minimum, you executor—know that your will exists and where it is located.

Your will should be left in a safe, accessible location. There is no one best place. It can be stored in a safe deposit box if you're sure your executor will have access to it after your death. Check with your bank about this. In many states, bank accounts, even joint tenancy bank accounts, of a person who died are "sealed" under state law until taxing authorities make an inventory, and are not therefore instantly accessible by your executor. If a safety deposit box might cause problems, you can store it in a safe place in your home or office, such as fireproof metal box.

Despite good intentions, it is often hard to find a will at death, and even harder to find other types of important personal property such as bank books and insurance policies. One good way to save your loved ones the misery of searching for your will and other important papers when they are already dealing with the grief of losing you is to make a clear record of your will and all other property, its location as well as the location of any ownership documents.[1] Also, in some states, such as Ohio and Texas, the local court clerk's office will store your will for a small fee.

What about copies of your will? Some people like to prepare more than one signed and exe - cuted original of their will in case one is lost or somehow inaccessible. While in most states the preparation and execution of duplicate originals (each one must be separately typed, signed and witnessed—you can't use photocopies) is legal, I strongly advise against it. If you later decide to change your will by adding a codicil, you have to change every original. This can be a burden. Or, worse, you might forget one or more of the duplicate original wills, and wind up changing some but not others, thus creating a confusing mess and potentially a legal disaster.

If you decide it's wise, you can give unsigned photocopies of your original will to people who you want to know of its contents, such as your executor, spouse or children. These copies, of course, are not legal wills, but are provided for information only. On the other hand, your will is your own business. You don't have to reveal its contents to anyone, even your witnesses. Giving close family members or other loved ones a summary of your will may be a good idea if all is peace and harmony, but there are sometimes lots of obvious practical reasons not to.

B. Don't Alter Your Will After You Sign It

Once you've prepared your will by using Nolo's Will Book, it is extremely important that you not alter it by inserting handwritten or typed additions or changes. Doing so will very probably invalidate your entire will. The laws of most states require that any additions or changes in a will, even clerical ones, be done in a formal way. This means either making a new signed and witnessed will, or adding a witnessed codicil (formal addition) to the existing one (see Section D below).

---

[1]*Your Family Records: How to Preserve Personal, Financial and Legal History* by Pladsen & Clifford (Nolo Press) offers one good way to do this.

C. Revising and Updating Your Will

There's no blanket rule covering when you should make a new will or add a formally-witnessed codicil. By now it should be clear to you that what your will contains is heavily dependent on circumstances. The state of your residence, your marital status, the property you own, whether you have (minor) children, and whether a child predeceases you, leaving children of his or her own, are all examples of variables that determine what should be included in your will. As these or other variables change, you will want to update your will.

Simple changes, such as a change of one beneficiary, the addition of a gift, or a change in an executor or alternate executor, can be accomplished by codicil (see Section D below). More exten-sive changes require revocation of your existing will and creation of a new one. You should definitely consider making a new will:

• If you change your mind about who you want to have a significant portion of your property.

• If you are married and move from a community property state to a common law property state, or vice versa. For a list of which states fall into which category, see Chapter 4, Section D. The reason you may need a new will in this circumstance is that community property and com-mon law property states view the ownership of property by married couples differently. This means the amount of property both you and your spouse have to leave may change if you move from one type of state to the other. Of course, if you plan to leave all or the bulk of your property to your spouse, this change will probably not have any real significance. If you move from one community property state or one common law state to another in the same category, it is probab-ly not necessary for you to change your will.

• If your marital status changes, especially if you marry after making your will. If you don't do this, your new spouse will automatically inherit a share of the property which may be different than you would have wished.

• If you have or adopt children. Each time a child is born or legally adopted into your family, you should review your will. The new child should be named in your new will and provided for according to your wishes. If you don't do this, the child will automatically be entitled to a share which may be different than you would have wished (see Chapter 7, Section D).

• If any of your children die before you, leaving children of his or her own. As I discuss in Chapter 7, these children (your grandchildren) may be entitled to receive a share of your estate (in some states) unless they receive property under the will or you have specifically disinherited them.

• If one of your children dies.

• If any of your beneficiaries die, and you haven't named an alternate beneficiary. If a benefi-ciary you have named to receive either a specific gift or the residue dies before you, check your will to be sure it reflects your current desires. Do you still want the alternate beneficiary to receive that gift? If you didn't name an alternate in the first place, do you want the gift to go to the residu-ary beneficiary? If not, change your will.

• If the property you leave in your will either expands or shrinks substantially after you've made out your will. In this case you should review your will to make sure it realistically reflects your current situation. This is especially true if there are changes in your ownership of real estate or expensive personal property items. For example, if you leave your 1985 Cadillac to your son and then trade it in and buy a 1987 Buick, your son will get nothing, unless you update your will.

On the other hand, if you leave your son "my car," he will get whatever car you own at your death, even though it is a different one than you owned when you made your will.

• If the persons you named as guardian or trustee for your children are no longer available to serve. These person(s) may move away, become disabled, or simply turn out to be not the kind of people you wish to care for your children or their property should this become necessary. If so, you will want to make a new will naming somebody more suitable.

• If the person(s) you named as your executor is no longer able to serve.

As you know, the executor of your estate is the person charged with making sure your wishes are faithfully complied with. You may discover that the person or institution you originally named would really not be the best person for this task. For example, if you originally named your spouse, who has subsequently become seriously ill, you may want to substitute one of your children. If so, you should write a new will and change executors.

D. Making Simple Changes in Your Will by Codicil

You can make simple changes in your will by means of a "codicil"—the legal name for a written amendment to the terms of a will, made after the original will has been witnessed and signed. Codicils are frequently used for minor matters such as changes of individual gifts. In a codicil, the will writer can revoke a clause in the will he wants to change and then adds a new clause, or the will writer can simply add a new provision, such as making a new specific personal property gift.

Example: Assume the will writer's brother, Jim, died, and the will writer wants to give the player piano he left to Jim to Jim's son, Fred.

"1. I revoke the provision of Clause 4 of my will leaving my player piano to my brother Jim and add the following as new provision to Clause f: I give my player piano to my nephew, Fred Jones, or, if he fails to survive me, to Jerry Johnston."

Example: The will writer buys a new gold necklace which she wants to leave to her favorite niece, Maria:

"I add the following new provision to Clause 4 of my will:

• I give my gold necklace to my niece, Maria Wallace, or, if she fails to survive me by 45 days, to Tom Wallace."

Again, if a major revision of the will is desired, don't use a codicil. A will which has been substantially re-written by a codicil is a confusing document and awkward to read. It may not be clear what the relationship of the codicil to the original will provision means. For major revi-sions, draft a new will and revoke the old one.

A codicil, being a sort of legal "P.S." to the will, must be executed with all of the formalities of a will which were discussed in Chapter 13. This means that the codicil must be typed, then dated and signed by you in front of three witnesses. These witnesses don't have to be the same people who witnessed the will, but it's advisable to use them if they're available. As with your original witnesses, these should not be named as beneficiaries in your will. If your will is "self-proved" with a notarized affidavit, another affidavit for the codicil should also be executed. Once the codicil is completed, it should be stored with the original will.

Important: Be sure anyone with an unsigned copy of your will receives an unsigned copy of the codicil. This may be a nuisance, but will prevent confusion, or even conflict, later. The codicil does not have to be made part of the signature page of the original will. It must, however, refer to that will. This can be simply accomplished by labeling the codicil document "first codicil of the will of _[your name]_ , dated _[giving date will was originally prepared]_ ." The entire will is now considered to have been prepared as of the date of the codicil.

E. Codicil Form

Following is a sample form you can use or adapt if it becomes necessary to make a codicil to your will. To use this form, follow the instructions for completing your draft will contained in Chapter 11, Section B: fill in the blanks, cross out all instructional language, and delete unwanted clauses. Then have the codicil form typed for you and your witnesses' signatures. If you need a self-proving affidavit, use the same form and follow the same instructions found in Section D of Chapter 13.

FIRST CODICIL TO THE WILL
OF

_____
your name

I, _____, a resident of
your name

_____, _____,
county   state

declare this to be the first codicil to my will dated _____, 19____.

FIRST: I revoke the provision of Clause _____, of my will which provided

_____
(Include the exact language you wish to revoke)

_____.

_____

_____

and substitute the following : (Add whatever is desired.)

_____

_____

_____

_____

SECOND: I add the following provision to Clause _____: (Add whatever is desired.)

_____

_____

_____

THIRD: In all other respects I confirm and republish my will dated _____

_____, 19___.

Dated _____,19___   _____
your name

I subscribe my name to this codicil this _____ day of _____ , 19__,

at _____, _____, _____,
　　　　　　city　　　　　　　　　　　　county　　　　　　　　　state

and do hereby declare that I sign and execute this codicil willingly, that I execute it as my

free and voluntary act for the purposes therein expressed, and that I am of the age of

majority or otherwise legally empowered to make a codicil and under no constraint or

undue influence.

_____
　　　　　　　　　　　　　　　your signed name

On this _____ day of _____ , 19 _____,

_____ declared to us, the undersigned,
　　　　　　　　your name

that this instrument was the codicil to _____ will and requested us to act as witnesses
　　　　　　　　　　　　　　　　　　　his/her

to it. _____ thereupon signed this codicil in our presence, all of us being present at
　　　　he/she

the same time. We now, at _____ request, in _____ presence, and in the
　　　　　　　　　　　　　his/her　　　　　　　his/her

presence of each other, subscribe our names as witnesses and declare we understand

this to be _____ codicil and that to be best of our knowledge _____ is of the age
　　　　　　his/her　　　　　　　　　　　　　　　　　　　　　　he/she

of majority, or is otherwise legally empowered to make a codicil and under no constraint or

undue influence.

We declare under penalty of perjury that the foregoing is true and correct.

_____ residing at _____

_____

_____ residing at _____

_____

_____ residing at _____

_____

F. Revocation of Your Will

Anyone who writes a will should understand how it can be revoked. There are only two ways: first, by deliberate act of the will writer; second, by operation of law. Let's look at each of these.

1. A Deliberate Act to Revoke a Will

A will writer who wants to revoke a prior will should do so by express written statement, as provided for in all wills in this book. In many states, an existing will (or codicil) is also revoked by being "burnt, torn, concealed, defaced, obliterated or destroyed" if the will writer intended to revoke it. This can be legally accomplished by someone other than the will writer at his or her direction. The problem with destroying a will, or having someone else do so, is that this only serves to revoke the will if you intend it to. After your death this can become a matter of contro - versy, especially if you have distributed copies of your original will. So if you want the satis - faction of destroying a revoked will, go right ahead, but be sure you've also revoked it in writing in your new will. This is the only good way to make your intention clear.

The revocation of a subsequent will does not revive an earlier one, unless the terms of the revocation state that it is the will writer's intent to revive the first will, or if the first will is "republished" (i.e., signed and witnessed anew). Thus, if Marguerite makes one will and then sometime later makes a second will expressly revoking the first will, the first will does not become valid if Marguerite tears up the second.

2. Revocation of a Will by Act of Law

This refers to spouses or children not mentioned in your will. As is discussed in Chapters 4 and 7, in most states spouses and children unmentioned in a will have statutory rights to a part of your property. So the law looks upon the will as being revoked as far as they are concerned, but not as to any other provisions. With a will drafted from the Will Book, you should not have to concern yourself with this, because if you followed instructions, you have mentioned your spouse and all your children in your will, and have either given something to each of your children, or expressly disinherited them.

Glossary

Abatement: Cutting back certain gifts under a will when it is necessary to create a fund to meet expenses, pay taxes, satisfy debts, or to have enough to take care of other bequests which are given a priority under law or under the will.

Acknowledgment: A statement in front of a person who is qualified to administer oaths (e.g., a Notary Public) that a document bearing your signature was actually signed by you.

Ademption: The failure of a specific bequest of property to take effect because the property is no longer owned by the testator at the time of his death.

Administration: (of an estate): The court-supervised distribution of the probate estate of a deceased person. The person who manages the distribution is called the executor if there is a will. If there is no will, this person is called the administrator. In some states, the person is called "personal representative" in either instance.

Adopted Children: Any person, whether an adult or a minor, who is legally adopted as the child of another in a court proceeding.

Adult: Any person over the age of 18. Most states allow all competent adults to make wills. A few, however, require you to be somewhat older (e.g., 19 or 21 to leave real estate).

Augmented Estate: A method used in a number of states following the common law ownership of property system to measure a person's estate for the purpose of determining whether a surviving spouse has been adequately provided for. Generally, the augmented estate consists of property left by the will plus certain property transferred outside of the will by such devices as gifts, joint tenancies and living trusts. In the states using this concept, a surviving spouse is gen-erally considered to be adequately provided for if he or she receives at least one-third of the augmented estate.

Beneficiary: A person or organization who is legally entitled to receive benefits under a legal document such as a will or trust. Except when very small estates are involved, beneficiaries of wills only receive their benefits after the will is examined and approved by the probate court. Beneficiaries of trusts receive their benefits as provided in the trust instrument.

Bequest: An old legal term for a will provision leaving personal property to a specified person or organization. In this book it is called a "gift."

Bond: A document guaranteeing that a certain among of money will be paid to those damaged if a person occupying a position of trust does not carry out his or her legal and ethical responsibili - ties. Thus, if an executor, trustee or guardian who is bonded (covered by a bond) wrongfully deprives a beneficiary of his or her property (say by blowing it during a trip in Las Vegas), the bonding company will replace it, up to the limits of the bond. Bonding companies, which are normally divisions of insurance companies, issue a bond in exchange for a premium (usually about 10% of the face amount of the bond). Under the Will Book, executors and guardians are appointed to serve without the necessity of purchasing a bond. This is because the cost of the bond would have to be paid out of the estate, and the beneficiaries would accordingly receive less. Under the Will Book, you should take care to select trustworthy people in the first place.

Children: For the purpose of the Will Book, children are: (1) the biological offspring of the will maker, (2) persons who were legally adopted by the will maker, (3) children born out of wed - lock if the will maker is the mother, (4) children born out of wedlock if the will maker is the father and has acknowledged the child as being his as required by the law of the particular state, or (5) children born to the will maker after the will is made, but before his or her death.

Codicil: A separate legal document that changes an existing will after it has been signed and properly witnessed.

Community and Separate Property: Eight states follow a system of marital property ownership called "community property," and Wisconsin has a very similar law. Very generally, all prop- erty acquired after marriage and before permanent separation is considered to belong equally to both spouses, except for gifts to and inheritances by one spouse, and, in some community property states, income from property owned by one spouse prior to marriage.

In most marriages, the main property accumulated is a family home, a retirement pension belong to one or both spouses, motor vehicles, a joint bank account, a savings account, and perhaps some stocks or bonds. So long as these were purchased during the marriage with the income earned by either spouse during the marriage, they are usually considered to be commu - nity property, unless the spouses have entered into an agreement to the contrary. If the property was purchased with the separate property of a spouse, it is separate property, unless it has been given to the community by gift or agreement.

If separate property and community property are mixed together (commingled) in a bank account and expenditures made from this bank account, the goods purchased will usually be treated as community property unless they can be specifically linked with the separate property (this is called "tracing").

Under the law of community property states, a surviving spouse automatically receives one- half of all community property. The other spouse has no legal power to affect this portion by will or otherwise. Thus, the property which a testator actually leaves by will consists of his or her separate property and one-half of the community property.

Conditional Gift: A gift which only passes under certain specified conditions or upon the occur - rence of a specific event. For example, if you leave property to Aunt Millie provided she is living in Cincinnati when you die, and otherwise to Uncle Fred, you have made a "conditional gift." The Will Book does not encourage or provide clauses for conditional bequests.

Custodian: A person named to care for property left to a minor under the Uniform Gifts (or Transfers) to Minor's Act.

Death Taxes: Taxes levied on the property of a person who died. Federal Death Taxes are called Estate Taxes. State Death Taxes (if any) go by various names, including Inheritance Tax.

Decedent: A person who has died.

Devise: An old English term for real estate given by a will. In this book, it is called a "gift."

Domicile: The state, or country, where one has his or her primary home.

Dower and Curtesy: The right of a surviving spouse to receive or enjoy the use of a set portion of the deceased spouse's property (usually one-third to one-half) in the event the surviving spouse is not left at least that share and chooses to take against the will. Dower refers to the title which a surviving wife gets, while curtesy refers to what a man receives. Until recently, these amounts differed in a number of states. However, since discrimination on the basis of sex is now considered to be illegal in most cases, states generally provide the same benefits regardless of sex.

Encumbrances: Debts (e.g., taxes, mechanics liens, judgment liens) and loans (e.g., mortgages, deeds of trust, security interests) which use property as collateral for payment of the debt or loan are considered to encumber the property because they must be paid off before title to the property can pass from one owner to the next. Generally, the value of a person's ownership in such property (called the "equity") is measured by the market value of the property less the sum of all encumbrances.

Estate: Generally, all the property you own when you die. There are different ways to measure your estate, depending on whether you are concerned with tax reduction (the taxable estate), probate avoidance (the probate estate), or net worth (the net estate).

Estate Planning: The art of dying with the smallest taxable estate and probate estate possible while continuing to prosper when you're alive and yet passing your property to your loved ones with a minimum of fuss and expense.

Estate Taxes: Federal taxes imposed on your property as it passes from the dead to the living. The federal government exempts $600,000 in 1987 and thereafter. Also, all property left to a sur - viving spouse is exempt under the marital exemption. Taxes are only imposed on property actually owned by you at the time of your death. Thus, estate planning techniques designed to reduce taxes usually concentrate on the legal transfer of ownership of your property while you are living, to minimize the amount of such property you own at your death.

Equity: The difference between the fair market value of your real and personal property and the amount you still owe on it, if any.

Executor: The person named in your will to manage your estate, deal with the probate court, collect your assets and distribute them as you have specified. In some states this person is called the "personal representative." If you die without a will, the probate court will appoint such a person., who is then called the "administrator" of the estate.

Financial Guardian: See **Guardian of the Minor's Property.**

Gifts: As used in the Will Book (except in Chapter 8 on estate planning), all property you leave to people, or organizations, on your death. A specific gift means an identified piece of property given to an inheritor.

Guardian of the Minor's Property: Termed "property guardian" in this book. The person (or institution) appointed or selected in your will to care for property of your minor child. Also sometimes called "the Guardian of the Minor's Estate," or "Financial Guardian." Usually the same person will serve as guardian of the person and property guardian. However, it is also possible to split these tasks.

Guardian of the Person: An adult appointed or selected to care for a minor child in the event no biological or adoptive parent (legal parent) of the child is able to do so. If one legal parent is alive when the other dies, however, the child will automatically go to that parent, unless the best interests of the child require something different, or (in some states) the court finds the child would suffer detriment.

Heirs: Persons who are entitled by law to inherit your estate if you don't leave a will, and any person or institution named in your will.

Holographic Will: A will that is completely handwritten by the person making it. While legal in many states, it is never advised except as a last resort.

Inherit: To receive property from one who dies.

Inheritors: Persons or organizations who you leave property to.

Inter Vivos Trusts: See **Living Trusts.**

Intestate: To die without a will.

Intestate Succession: The method by which property is distributed when a person fails to distribute it in a will. In such cases, the law of each state provides that the property be distributed in certain shares to the closest surviving relatives. In most states, these are a surviving spouse, children, parents, siblings, nieces and nephews, and next of kin, in that order. The intestate succession laws are also used in the event an heir is found to be pretermitted (i.e., not mentioned or otherwise provided for in the will).

Joint Tenancy: A way to take title to jointly owned real or personal property. When two or more people own property as joint tenants, and one of the owners dies, the other owners automat - ically become owners of the deceased owner's share. Thus, if a parent and child own a house a joint tenants, and the parent dies, the child automatically becomes full owner. Because of this "right of survivorship," a joint tenancy interest in property does not go through probate, or, put another way, is not part of the probate estate. Instead it goes directly to the surviving joint tenant(s) once some tax and transfer forms are completed.

Placing property in joint tenancy is therefore a common tool used in estate planning designed to avoid probate. However, when property is placed in joint tenancy, a gift is made to any persons who become owners as a result. Thus, if Tom owns a house and places it in joint tenancy with Karen, Tom will have made a gift to Karen equal to one-half the house's value. This may have gift tax consequences.

Living Trusts: Trusts set up while a person is alive and which remain under the control of that person during the remainder of his or her life. Also referred to as "inter vivos trusts," living trusts are an excellent way to minimize the value of property passing through probate. This is because they enable people (called "trustors") to specify that money or other property (called the "trust corpus") will pass directly to their beneficiaries at the time of their death, free of probate, and yet allow the trustors to continue to control the property during their lifetime and even end the trust or change the beneficiaries if they wish.

Marriage: A specific status conferred on a couple by the state. In most states, it is necessary to file papers with a county clerk and have a marriage ceremony conducted by authorized individuals in order to be married. However, in a minority of states called "common law marriage" states you may be considered married if you have lived together for a certain period of time and intended to be husband and wife. These states are: Alabama, Colorado, District of Columbia, Georgia, Idaho, Iowa, Kansas, Montana, Oklahoma, Pennsylvania, Rhode Island, South Carolina and Texas.

Unless you are considered legally married in the state where you claim your marriage occurred, you are not married for purposes of the Will Book.

Marital Exemption: A deduction allowed by the federal estate tax law for all property passed to a surviving spouse. This deduction (which really acts like an exemption) allows anyone, even a billionaire, to pass his or her entire estate to a surviving spouse without any tax at all. This might be a good idea if the surviving spouse is young and in good health.

If the surviving spouse is likely to die in the near future, however, your tax problems will very likely be made worse by relying on the marital exemption. This is because the second spouse to die will normally benefit from no marital deduction, which means the combined estate, less the standard estate tax exemption, will be taxed at a fairly high rate. For this reason, many older couples with adequate resources do not leave large amounts of property to each other, but rather, leave it directly to their children so that each can qualify for a separate tax exemption.

Minor: In most states, persons under 18 years of age. A minor is not permitted to make certain types of decisions (e.g., enter into most contracts). All minors are required to be under the care of a competent adult (parent or guardian) unless they qualify as emancipated minors (in the military, married, or living independently with court permission). This also means that prop‑ erty left to a minor must be handled by a guardian or trustee until the minor becomes an adult under the laws of the state.

Net Taxable Estate: The value of all your property at death less all encumbrances and your other liabilities.

Personal Property: All property other than land and buildings attached to land. Cars, bank accounts, wages, securities, a small business, furniture, insurance policies, jewelry, pets, season baseball tickets, etc., are all personal property.

Power of Attorney: A legal document where you authorize someone else to act for you. A durable power of attorney allows someone to act for you if you become incapacitated, to make health care and financial decisions for you.

Pretermitted Heir: A child (or the child of a deceased child) who is either not named or (in some states) not provided for in a will. Most states presume that persons want their children to inherit. Accordingly, children, or the children of a child who has died before the person making the will (the "testator") who are not mentioned or provided for in the will (even by as little as

$1.00) are automatically given a share of the estate unless such children are specifically disinherited in the will.

Probate: The court proceeding in which: (1) the authenticity of your will (if any) is established, (2) your executor or administrator is appointed, (3) your debts and taxes are paid, (4) your heirs are identified, and (5) your property in your probate estate is distributed according to your will (if there is a will).

Probate Estate: All of your property that will pass through probate. Generally, this means all property owned by you at your death less any property that has been placed in joint tenancy, a living trust, a bank account trust, or in life insurance.

Probate Fees: Because probate is so laden with legal formalities, it is usually necessary to hire an attorney to handle it. Under the law of some states, an attorney handling probate is entitled to be paid a percentage of the overall value of the probate estate. This can mean that the attorney will take a substantial fee of the estate before it is distributed to the heirs.

Proving a Will: Getting a probate court to accept the fact after your death that your will really is your will. In many states this can be done simply by introducing a properly executed will. In others, it is necessary to produce one or more witnesses (or affidavits of such witnesses) in court, or offer some proof of the testator's handwriting. Having the testator and witnesses sign a sworn statement (affidavit) before a notary public stating that all will-making formalities were complied with usually allows the will to "prove" itself without the need for the witnesses to testify, or other evidence.

Quasi-Community Property: A rule in Idaho and California that requires all property acquired by people during their marriage in other states to be treated as community property at their death in the event the couple has moved to one of these states.

Real Estate: A term used by the Will Book as a synonym for "real property."

Real Property: All land and items attached to the land, such as buildings, houses, stationary mobile homes, fences and trees as considered as "real property" or "real estate." All property which is not "real property" is personal property.

Residue, Residuary Estate: All property given by your will to your residuary beneficiary after all specific gifts of property (real and personal) have been made, i.e., "what's left."

Spouse: In the Will Book, your spouse is the person to whom you are legally married at the time you sign the will. If you later remarry, you will need to make a new will if you wish to leave property to your new spouse.

Taking Against the Will: The ability of a surviving spouse to choose a statutorily allotted share of the deceased spouse's estate instead of the share specified in his or her will. In most common law property states, the law provides for a surviving spouse to receive a minimum percentage of the other spouse's estate (commonly between one-third and one-half). If the deceased spouse leaves the surviving spouse less than this in, or outside of, the will, the surviving spouse may elect the statutory share instead of the will provision (i.e., take against the will). If the spouse chooses to accept the share specified in the will, it is called "taking under the will."

Taxable Estate: The portion of your estate that is subject to federal and/or state estate taxes.

Tenancy in Common: A way of jointly owning property in which each person's share passes to his/her heirs. The ownership shares need not be equal.

Testator: The person making the will.

Totten Trust (also called pay-on-death bank accounts): Simple bank trust account enabling the depositor to name a beneficiary to receive the fund in the account after the beneficiary dies.

Trust: A legal arrangement under which one person or institution (called a "trustee") controls property given by another person for the benefit of a third person (called a "beneficiary"). The property itself can be termed the "corpus" of the trust.

Uniform Gifts/Transfers to Minors Act: A series of statutes that provide standard guidelines for transferring property to minors. Enacted into law by most states, the Uniform Gifts (or Transfers) to Minors Act is used by Chapter 12 of the Will Book to govern how property left to minors other than your own children is handled.

Will: A legal document in which a person states various binding intentions about what he/she wants done after his/her death.

About the Author

Denis Clifford is a lawyer who specializes in estate planning, and has been involved in the developing uses of durable powers of attorney. He is the author of several Nolo Press books, including *Plan Your Estate: Wills, Probate Avoidance, Trusts & Taxes, The Power of Attorney Book* and *Your Family Records: How to Preserve Personal, Financial and Legal History*. A graduate of Columbia Law School, where he was an editor of *The Law Review*, he has practiced law in various ways, and became convinced that people can do much of the legal work they need themselves.

About the Illustrator

Mari Stein is a free lance illustrator and writer. Her published work has been eclectic, covering a wide range of subjects: humor, whimsy, health education, juvenile, fables and Yoga. Among the books she has written and illustrated are "Some Thoughts for my Friends," and "VD The Love Epidemic." She has also illustrated childrens' books, textbooks, magazine articles, and a book of poetry. She has illustrated many books for Nolo Press. She works out of a studio in her Pacific Palisades home, where she lives with her dogs and rabbits, cultivates roses, and teaches Yoga.

Will Paper Kit

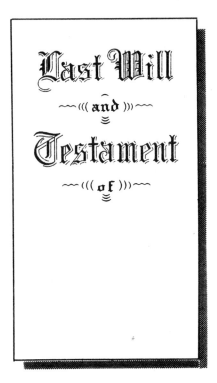

To give your will a more formal look, the **Will Paper Kit** contains the standard will preparation outfit used by many lawyers. The legality of your will is not affected by what kind of paper that you use, only the appearance is enhanced.

The **Will Paper Kit** includes:

- 3 Will envelopes with gummed seals
- 3 heavy backing sheets to staple your will to
- 3 will title pages with the heading "Last Will and Testament"
- 36 continuation sheets (all paper is 25% rag)

Just send $6.95 + $1.50 (California residents) or $2.00 (all other residents) postage to:

Will Paper Kit
Nolo Press
950 Parker St.
Berkeley, CA 94710

nolo
self-help law books

BUSINESS & FINANCE

California Incorporator
By attorney Mancuso and Legisoft, Inc. About half of the small California corporations formed today are done without the services of a lawyer. This easy-to-use software program lets you do the paperwork with minimum effort. Just answer the questions on the screen, and *California Incorporator* will print out the 35-40 pages of documents you need to make your California corporation legal.
California Edition $129.00

How To Form Your Own Corporation
By attorney Mancuso. Provides all the forms, Bylaws, Articles, minutes of meeting, stock certificates and instructions necessary to form your small profit corporation. Includes a thorough discussion of the practical and legal aspects of incorporation, including the tax consequences.
California Edition $29.95
Texas Edition $21.95
New York Edition $19.95
Florida Edition $19.95

The Non-Profit Corporation Handbook
By attorney Mancuso. Includes all the forms, Bylaws, Articles, minutes, and instructions you need to form a non-profit corporation. Step-by-step instructions on how to choose a name, draft Articles and Bylaws, attain favorable tax status. Thorough information on federal tax exemptions, which groups outside of California will find particularly useful.
California only $24.95

**The California Professional
Corporation Handbook**
By attorneys Mancuso and Honigsberg. In California a number of professions must fulfill special requirements when forming a corporation. Among them are lawyers, dentists, doctors and other health professionals, accountants and certain social workers. This book contains detailed information on the special requirements of every profession and all the forms and instructions necessary to form a professional corporation.
California only $29.95

Marketing Without Advertising
By Phillips and Rasberry. A creative and practical guide that shows small business people how to avoid wasting money on advertising. The authors, experienced business consultants, show how to implement an ongoing marketing plan to tell potential and current customers that yours is a quality business worth trusting, recommending and coming back to.
National Edition $14.00

Billpayers' Rights
By attorney Warner. Complete information on bankruptcy, student loans, wage attachments, dealing with bill collectors and collection agencies, credit cards, car repossessions, homesteads, child support and much more.
California only $14.95

Bankruptcy: Do-It-Yourself
By attorney Kosel. Tells you exactly what bankruptcy is all about and how it affects your credit rating, property and debts, with complete details on property you can keep under the state and federal exempt property rules. Shows you step-by-step how to do it yourself; comes with all necessary forms and instructions.
National Edition $17.95

The Partnership Book
By attorneys Clifford and Warner. When two or more people join to start a small business, one of the most basic needs is to establish a solid, legal partnership agreement. This book supplies a number of sample agreements which you can use as is. Buy-out clauses, unequal sharing of assets, and limited partnerships are all discussed in detail.
National Edition $18.95

**Chapter 13: The Federal Plan
to Repay Your Debts**
By attorney Kosel. This book allows an individual to develop and carry out a feasible plan to pay most of his/her debts over a three-year period. Chapter 13 is an alternative to straight bankruptcy and yet it still means the end of creditor harassment, wage attachments and other collection efforts. Comes complete with all necessary forms and worksheets.
National Edition $17.95

Small Time Operator
By Kamoroff, C.P.A.. Shows you how to start and operate your small business, keep your books, pay your taxes and stay out of trouble. Comes complete with a year's supply of ledgers and worksheets designed especially for small businesses, and contains invaluable information on permits, licenses, financing, loans, insurance, bank accounts, etc. Published by Bell Springs.
National Edition $10.95

Start-Up Money: How to Finance Your Small Business
By Business Consultant McKeever. For anyone about to start a business or revamp an existing one, this book shows how to write a business plan, draft a loan package and find sources of small business finance.
National Edition $15.95

Getting Started as an Independent Paralegal (two audio cassette tapes)
By attorney Warner. In these two audiotapes, about three hours in all, Ralph Warner explains how to set up and run an independent paralegal business and how to market your services. He also discusses in detail how to avoid charges of unauthorized practice of law.
National 1st Edition $24.95

The Independent Paralegal's Handbook: How to Provide Legal Services Without Going to Jail
By attorney Warner. More and more nonlawyers are opening legal typing services to help people prepare their own papers for divorce, bankruptcy, incorporation, eviction, etc. Called independent paralegals, these legal pioneers pose much the same challenge to the legal establishment as midwives do to conventional medicine. Written by Nolo Press co-founder Ralph Warner, who established one of the first divorce typing services in 1973, this controversial book is sure to become the bible of the new movement aimed at delivering routine legal services to the public at a reasonable price.
National Edition $12.95

COPYRIGHTS & PATENTS

Legal Care for Your Software
By attorney Remer. Shows the software programmer how to protect his/her work through the use of trade secret, trademark, copyright, patent and, most especially, contractual laws and agreements. This book is full of forms and instructions that give programmers the hands-on information they need.
International Edition $29.95

Intellectual Property Law Dictionary
By attorney Elias. "Intellectual Property" includes ideas, creations and inventions. The Dictionary is designed for inventors, authors, programmers, journalists, scientists and business people who must understand how the law affects the ownership and control of new ideas and technologies. Divided into sections on: Trade Secrets, Copyrights, Trademarks, Patents and Contracts. More than a dictionary, it places terms in context as well as defines them.
National Edition $17.95

How to Copyright Software
By attorney Salone. Shows the serious programmer or software developer how to protect his or her programs through the legal device of copyright.
International Edition $24.95

Patent It Yourself
By attorney Pressman. Complete instructions on how to do a patent search and file for a patent in the U.S. Also covers how to choose the appropriate form of protection (copyright, trademark, trade secret, etc.), how to evaluate salability of inventions, patent prosecution, marketing, use of the patent, foreign filing, licensing, etc. Tear-out forms are included
National Edition $29.95

Inventor's Notebook
By Fred Grissom and attorney David Pressman. The best protection for your patent is adequate records. The Inventor's Notebook provides forms, instructions, references to relevant areas of patent law, a bibliography of legal and non-legal aids, and more. It helps you document the activities that are normally part of successful independent inventing.
National 1st Edition $19.95

ESTATE PLANNING, WILLS & PROBATE

Plan Your Estate: Wills, Probate Avoidance, Trusts and Taxes
By attorney Clifford. Comprehensive information on making a will, alternatives to probate, planning to limit inheritance and estate taxes, living trusts, and providing for family and friends.
California Edition $15.95

Nolo's Simple Will Book
By attorney Clifford. This book will show you how to draft a will without a lawyer in any state except Louisiana. Covers all the basics, including what to do about children, whom you can designate to carry out your wishes, and how to comply with the technical legal requirements of each state. Includes examples and many alternative clauses from which to choose.
National Edition $14.95
with cassette $19.95

WillMaker
—a software/book package
By Legisoft. Use your computer to prepare and update your own valid will. A manual provides help in areas such as tax planning and probate avoidance. Runs on the Apple II family, IBM PC and compatibles, Commodore, Macintosh .
National Edition $59.95
Commodore Edition $39.95

How to Probate an Estate
By Nissley. Forms and instructions necessary to settle a California resident's estate after death. This book deals with joint tenancy and community property transfers as well as showing you how to actually probate an estate, step-by-step. The book is aimed at the executor, administrator or family member who will have the actual responsibility to settle the estate.
California Edition $24.95

LANDLORD/TENANT

Tenants' Rights
By attorneys Moskovitz, Warner and Sherman. Discusses everything tenants need to know in order to protect themselves: getting deposits returned, breaking a lease, getting repairs made, using Small Claims Court, dealing with an unscrupulous landlord, forming a tenants' organization, etc. Sample Fair-to-Tenants lease, rental agreements, and unlawful detainer answer forms.
California Edition $14.95

The Landlord's Law Book: Rights and Responsibilities
By attorneys Brown and Warner. Now, for the first time, there is an accessible, easy to understand law book written specifically for landlords. Covers the areas of discrimination, insurance, tenants' privacy, leases, security deposits, rent control, liability, and rent with-holding.
California only $24.95

The Landlord's Law Book: Evictions
By attorney Brown. This is the most comprehensive manual available on how to do each step of an eviction, and the only one to deal with rent control cities and contested evictions including how to represent yourself in court if necessary. All the required forms, with directions on how to complete and file them, are included. Vol. 1 covers Rights and Responsibilities.
California only $24.95

Landlording
By Robinson (Express Press). Written for the conscientious landlord or landlady, this comprehensive guide discusses maintenance and repairs, getting good tenants, how to avoid evictions, record keeping and taxes.
National Edition $17.95

REAL ESTATE

All About Escrow
(Express Press) By Gadow. This book gives you a good understanding of what your escrow officer should be doing for you. Includes advice about inspections, financing, condominiums and cooperatives.
National Edition $12.95

The Deeds Book
By attorney Randolph. Adding or removing a name from a deed, giving up interest in community property at divorce, putting a house in joint tenancy to avoid probate, all these transactions require a change in the way title to real estate is held. This book shows you how to choose the right deed, fill it out and record it.
California Edition $15.95

Homebuyers: Lambs to the Slaughter
By attorney Bashinsky (Menasha Ridge Press). Written by a lawyer/broker, this book describes how sellers, agents, lenders and lawyers are out to fleece you, the buyer, and advises how to protect your interests.
National Edition $12.95

For Sale By Owner
By Devine. The average California home sold for $130,000 in 1986. That meant the average seller paid $7800 in broker's commissions. This book will show you how to sell your own home and save the money. All the background information and legal technicalities are included to help you do the job yourself and with confidence.
California Edition $24.95

Homestead Your House
By attorney Warner. Under the California Homestead Act, you can file a Declaration of Homestead and thus protect your home from being sold to satisfy most debts. This book explains this simple and inexpensive procedure and includes all the forms and instructions. Contains information on exemptions for mobile homes and houseboats.
California only $8.95

RESEARCHING THE LAW

California Civil Code
(West Publishing) Statutes covering a wide variety of topics, rights and duties in the landlord/tenant relationship, marriage and divorce, contracts, transfers of real estate, consumer credit, power of attorney, and trusts.
California only $17.00

California Code of Civil Procedure
(West Publishing) Statutes governing most judicial and administrative procedures: unlawful detainer (eviction) proceedings, small claims actions, homestead procedures, wage garnishments, recording of liens, statutes of limitation, court procedures, arbitration, and appeals.
California only $17.00

Legal Research: How to Find and Understand the Law
By attorney Elias. A hands-on guide to unraveling the mysteries of the law library. For paralegals, law students, consumer activists, legal secretaries, business and media people. Shows exactly how to find laws relating to specific cases or legal questions, interpret statutes and regulations, find and research cases, understand case citations and Shepardize them.
National Edition $14.95

Family Law Dictionary
By attorneys Leonard and Elias. A national reference guide containing straightforward explanations and examples of an area of law which touches all of our lives. The book is extremely useful for people who want to know how the laws of marriage, divorce, cohabitation and having children affect them, and for legal practitioners in the area of family law.
National Edition $13.95

How to Do Your Own Divorce
By attorney Sherman. This is the original "do-your-own-law" book. It contains tear-out copies of all the court forms required for an uncontested dissolution, as well as instructions for certain special forms.
California Edition $14.95
Texas Edition $12.95

A Legal Guide for Lesbian/Gay Couples
By attorneys Curry and Clifford. Here is a book that deals specifically with legal matters of lesbian and gay couples: raising children (custody, support, living with a lover), buying property together, wills, etc. and comes complete with sample contracts and agreements.
National Edition $17.95

The Living Together Kit
By attorneys Ihara and Warner. A legal guide for unmarried couples with information about buying or sharing property, the Marvin decision, paternity statements, medical emergencies and tax consequences. Contains a sample will and Living Together Contract.
National Edition $17.95

California Marriage and Divorce Law
By attorneys Ihara and Warner. This book contains invaluable information for married couples and those considering marriage or remarriage on community and separate property, names, debts, children, buying a house, etc. Includes prenuptial contracts, a simple will, probate avoidance information and an explanation of gift and inheritance taxes. Discusses "secret marriage" and "common law" marriage.
California only $15.95

Social Security, Medicare & Pensions: A Sourcebook for Older Americans
By attorney Matthews & Berman. The most comprehensive resource tool on the income, rights and benefits of Americans over 55. Includes detailed information on social security, retirement rights, Medicare, Medicaid, supplemental security income, private pensions, age discrimination, as well as a thorough explanation of social security legislation.
National Edition $14.95

How to Modify & Collect Child Support in California
By attorneys Matthews, Segal and Willis. California court awards for child support have radically increased in the last two years. This book contains the forms and instructions to obtain the benefits of this change without a lawyer and collect support directly from a person's wages or benefits, if necessary.
California only $17.95

How to Adopt Your Stepchild
By Zagone. Shows you how to prepare all the legal forms; includes information on how to get the consent of the natural parent and how to conduct an "abandonment" proceeding. Discusses appearing in court and making changes in birth certificates.
California only $19.95

The Power of Attorney Book
By attorney Clifford. Covers the process which allows you to arrange for someone else to protect your rights and property should you become incapable of doing so. Discusses the advantages and drawbacks and gives complete instructions for establishing a power of attorney yourself.
National Edition $17.95

How to Change Your Name
By attorneys Loeb and Brown. Changing one's name is a very simple procedure. Using this book, you can file the necessary papers yourself, saving $200 to $300 in attorney's fees. Comes complete with all forms and instructions for the court petition method or this simpler usage method.
California only $14.95

Your Family Records: How to Preserve Personal, Financial and Legal History
By Pladsen and attorney Clifford. Helps you organize and record all sorts of items that will affect you and your family when death or disability occur, e.g., where to find your will and deed to the house. Includes information about probate avoidance, joint ownership of property and genealogical research. Space is provided for financial and legal records.
National Edition $14.95

RULES & TOOLS

Make Your Own Contract

By attorney Elias. Provides tear-out contracts, with instructions, for non-commercial use. Covers lending money, selling or leasing personal property (e.g., cars, boats), leasing and storing items (with friends, neighbors), doing home repairs, and making deposits to hold personal property pending final payment. Includes an appendix listing all the contracts found in Nolo books.

National Edition $12.95

The Criminal Records Book

By attorney Siegel. Takes you step-by-step through the procedures available to get your records sealed, destroyed or changed. Detailed discussion on your criminal record what it is, how it can harm you, how to correct inaccuracies, marijuana possession records and juvenile court records.

California only $14.95

Everybody's Guide to Small Claims Court

By attorney Warner. Guides you step-by-step through the Small Claims procedure, providing practical information on how to evaluate your case, file and serve papers, prepare and present your case, and, most important, how to collect when you win. Separate chapters focus on common situations (landlord-tenant, automobile sales and repair, etc.).

National Edition $14.95
California Edition $14.95

Fight Your Ticket

By attorney Brown. A comprehensive manual on how to fight your traffic ticket. Radar, drunk driving, preparing for court, arguing your case to a judge, cross-examining witnesses are all covered.

California only $16.95

The People's Law Review

Edited by Warner. This is the first compendium of people's law resources ever published. Contains articles on mediation and the new "non-adversary" mediation centers, information on self-help law programs and centers (for tenants, artists, battered women, the disabled, etc.); and articles dealing with many common legal problems which show people how to do-it-themselves.

National Edition $8.95

How to Become a United States Citizen

By Sally Abel. Detailed explanation of the naturalization process. Includes step-by-step instructions from filing for naturalization to the final oath of allegiance. Includes a study guide on U.S. history and government. Text is written in both English and Spanish.

National Edition $12.95

Draft, Registration and The Law

By attorney Johnson. How it works, what to do, advice and strategies.

California only $9.95

JUST FOR FUN

Murder on the Air

By Ralph Warner and Toni Ihara. An unconventional murder mystery set in Berkeley, California. When a noted environmentalist and anti-nuclear activist is killed at a local radio station, the Berkeley violent crime squad swings into action. James Rivers, an unplugged lawyer, and Sara Tamura, Berkeley's first female murder squad detective, lead the chase. The action is fast, furious and fun. $5.95

29 Reasons Not to Go to Law School

By attorneys Ihara and Warner, with contributions by fellow lawyers and illustrations by Mari Stein. A humorous and irreverent look at the dubious pleasures of going to law school. 3rd Ed. $8.95

Poetic Justice

Edited by Jonathan & Edward Roth. A compendium of the funniest, meanest things ever said about lawyers with quotes from Lao-Tzu to Lenny Bruce. $8.95

self-help law books

ORDER FORM

Quantity	Title	Unit Price	Total

Prices subject to change

Subtotal _____

Tax (CA only): San Mateo, LA, & Bart Counties 6 1/2%
Santa Clara & Alameda 7%
All others 6%

Tax_____

Postage & Handling

No. of Books   Charge
1                $1.50
2-3 $2.00
4-5 $2.50
Over 5 add 5% of total before tax

Postage & Handling_____

Total_____

Please allow 3-5 weeks for delivery.
For faster service, add $1 for UPS delivery (no P.O. boxes, please).

Name_____

Address _____

_____

n VISA   n Mastercard

_____Exp._____

Signature_____

Phone (   )_____

ORDERS: Credit card information or a check may be sent t⌐

Nolo Press
950 Parker St.
Berkeley CA 94710

Use your credit card and our **800 lines** for faster service:

ORDERS ONLY
(M-F 9-5 Pacific Time)**:**

US:	**800-992-NOLO**
Outside (415) area **CA:**	**800-445-NOLO**
Inside (415) area **CA:**	**(415) 549-1976**

For general information call: **(415) 549-1976**

☐ Please send me a catalogue